LUJIAZUI FINANCIAL & TRADE ZONE YEARBOOK

2013 陆家嘴金融城年鉴

Abridged Version | 中英对照简缩版

上海三联书店
SHANGHAI JOINT PUBLISHING COMPANY

序言
PREFACE

A year of fruitful achievements

In 2012, Lujiazui Financial City accelerated its role in the development of an international financial center in Shanghai and further cemented its status as one of the city's most important business districts, in accordance with objectives outlined by the central government in the 12th Five-Year Plan. Additionally, Lujiazui boosted efforts to strengthen the local shipping, construction and financial-services industries. These successful initiatives bolstered the strength of the Lujiazui brand and bulwarked the dynamic local economy, laying a solid foundation for future growth.

Rising investment

As of the end of 2012, the Lujiazui Financial City had attracted the following capital amounts: registered domestic capital of 39.455 billion yuan, accounting for 37.29% of overall capital in the district; contractual foreign investment 2.113 billion U.S. dollars, accounting for 25.54% of overall investment in the district; actual foreign capital of 1.464 billion U.S. dollars, which helped form the financial capacity of 13.523 billion yuan, accounting for 30.31% of overall investment in the district; 19.063 billion yuan in fixed assets investment, accounting for 13.76% of overall investment in the district. In 2012, 662 licensed financial institutions were marking an increase over 5.1% over 2011 and comprising 92% of all newly licensed financial institutions in the Pudong New District and 60% in

2012年，陆家嘴金融城紧紧抓住推进上海国际金融中心的目标，按照"十二五"发展规划中确定的"打造上海国际金融中心建设的核心区、上海核心中央商务区的重要区域、具有重要影响的高端航运服务集聚区"的中心任务，围绕区委、区府关于"4+3"开发区要着力"强功能、促转型"的工作要求，大力发展区域经济，大力扶持重点产业，全力推进重点工程建设，不断优化综合配套环境，着力建设金融人才高地，大力推进金融城品牌建设，使陆家嘴金融城金融机构的集聚达到新的水平，产业功能有新的突破，经济贡献有新的提升，为实现金融城新一轮的发展打下了坚实的基础。

经济发展和产业集聚有新路径

截止到2012年底，陆家嘴金融城吸引注册内资394.55亿元，占新区37.29%；吸引合同外资21.13亿美元，占新区25.54%；实到外资14.64亿美元，占新区30.31%；形成新区地方财力135.23亿元，占新区24.59%；完成固定资产投资190.63亿元，占新区13.76%。引进持牌类金融机构662家，较上年增长5.1%，占浦东新区近

Shanghai overall. 18 of those financial institutions were foreign banks, accounting for 82% of all newly licensed foreign banks in Shanghai and half in China's total. Additionally, there were 31 new fund management companies, accounting for 86% of such firms overall in Shanghai and 40% nationally, 35 financial leasing companies, accounting for 38% of those in the Pudong New District and 30 percent in the city overall and 415 new equity investments (including venture capital), accounting for 54.11 percent of the overall number in Pudong. Lastly, 81 new regional headquarters of multinational companies were set up in Lujiazui, accounting for nearly 42% of the overall number of new headquarters set up in Pudong. 40 of them were investment companies and 41 management companies.

Projects of note

The following projects were under construction in Lujiazui in 2012: Shanghai Center, Shanghai International Financial Center, Lujiazui Financial City of Riverside, Century Metropolis, the Tangdong Headquarter base, New York University in Shanghai. Meanwhile, construction was completed on the South Riverside Bar Street, Bespoke Clothing Street, Lujiazui Food Plaza and North Riverside Cultural Corridor, comprising about 19,000 square meters of commercial facilities meanwhile the shuttle bus route No. 2 and 3 completed. Additionally, free"CMCC-LJZ" WIFI was installed to cover the area of "Little Lujiazui." At the same time, special apartments for working professionals in the area were opened, 13 new taxi stands and an integrated system to facilitate pedestrian traffic were

92%，占上海市 60%，其中外资法人银行 18 家，约占上海市的 82%，占全国的一半；基金管理公司 31 家，约占上海市的 86%，全国的 40%。融资租赁公司 35 家，占浦东的 38%、全市的 30%。股权投资公司（含创业投资）415 家，占浦东的 54.11%。累计引进跨国公司地区总部企业 81 家，占新区总数 193 家的 41.97%，其中，投资性公司 40 家，管理性公司 41 家。

综合环境配套和功能建设有新亮点

2012 年，上海中心、上海国际金融中心、陆家嘴滨江金融城、塘东总部基地、世纪大都会、上海纽约大学等重点工程正在抓紧建设。南滨江酒吧休闲街、成衣定制街、陆家嘴餐饮广场、北滨江文化长廊约 1.9 万平方米商业配套已建设完成。免费"CMCC-LJZ" WIFI 已覆盖小陆家嘴，金融城 2 路、3 路和人才公寓专线已经开通，13 个出租车扬招点和行人指示系统建设完成，方便了公众在金融城出行；调整与完善金融城白领便捷式餐饮点，缓解白领们"用餐难"问题。

installed to improve traffic flow in Lujiazui and mobile catering trucks were launched to provide more convenient dining options for the area's working professionals.

Robust growth

In 2012, the Pudong New Area experienced strong growth across the board, notably in its infrastructure, financial-services sector, small and medium-sized companies and state-owned enterprises. This robust economic growth boosted the overall standard of living for Pudong residents. Overall in 2012, the Pudong New Area added value in the financial sector was 106.9 billion yuan, an increase of 11.9% year on year and 1.1 percent higher than the increase rate in 2011, accounting for 43.6% of the city's financial industry value, 18 % of total district production and 29% of tertiary industry production.

New educational institutions and key policies

A number of new educational institutions were set up in Lujiazui in 2012, notably New York University Shanghai and the Jiaotong University Advanced Institute of Finance, Shanghai University of Finance and Economics. Overall, Lujiazui boosted the area's educational resources in cooperation with the Harvard Shanghai Center and Wharton. At the same time, to strengthen the area's professional talent pool, Lujiazui implemented the Finance Professional

金融业发展对地方经济增长贡献率有新提升

金融城充裕的金融资源为金融城内和浦东新区的中小微企业、国有企业的发展，基础设施的建设以及民生的改善发挥了重要作用，金融对经济增长的贡献率不断提升。2012 年全年，浦东新区实现金融业增加值 1069 亿元，同比增长 11.9%，增幅同比提高 1.1 个百分点，占全市金融业增加值的比重达 43.6%，占新区生产总值的 18%，占新区第三产业增加值的 29.9%，金融业的核心支柱产业地位进一步提高。

人才创新创业基地建设有新探索

上海纽约大学顺利落户陆家嘴，积极引进上海交大高级金融学院、上海财大等资源，加大教育资源的集聚，实现了陆家嘴的金融人才与哈佛大学上海中心、沃顿商学院等金融教育资源的互动，实现人才的可持续开发。与此同时，坚持以优化人才综合服务环境为抓手，帮助人才解决"急难愁"问题，通过《新区集聚金融人才实施办法》等政策的落地，对金融人才实施了奖励；建立金融人才医疗健康服务平台；实施了"631"补贴政策，降低金融城人才公寓的居住成本，受到了用人单位和人才的广泛欢迎。

Recruitment Policy, created a healthcare service platform for finance professionals and enacted the 631 subsidy policy to reduce the cost of living in the "Talent Apartments."

A rich past and bright future

Lujiazui had a number of other notable accomplishments in 2012. For instance, the First Financial Lujiazui Magazine was founded, to provide information about the financial-services industry to finance professionals. Additionally, Lujiazui set up the Lujiazui Financial City English website with the help of China Daily, released a short film "Morning Lujiazui," and installed more than 100 LED information screens throughout the district as well as new signage.

With our past achievements in mind, we look to the future with confidence. Lujiazui will concentrate its many resources to boost the construction of an international financial center in Shanghai in a sustainable manner. We are certain Lujiazui will not only continue to develop as a model district but will play a truly vanguard role in Shanghai's future development.

金融城品牌建设有新突破

与第一财经联合创办的面向专业群体的《陆家嘴》专业财经杂志，与中国日报联合创办面向海外投资者的陆家嘴金融城英文网站。创作完成微电影《Morning 陆家嘴》。有针对性地推动旨在强化金融城金融元素的相关工作，在陆家嘴明珠环、陆家嘴环路指示牌、巴士及站点等地设立 100 多块 LED 信息屏，传递正能量的同时引领金融城白领的时尚生活方式，营造良好的金融文化氛围。

回顾过去，展望未来，我们对陆家嘴金融城建设充满信心，我们将继续以"机构集聚、空间扩展和环境优化"为目标，促转型、强功能，积极发挥上海国际金融中心建设的排头兵和主力军作用，共同为陆家嘴新一轮的发展建设努力奋斗！

CONTENTS
目录

 **4** EXHIBITIONS 会展    **5** PLANNED CONSTRUCTION 规划建设    **6** SUPPORTING ENVIRONMENT 配套环境    **7** CULTURE 文化

CONTENTS
目录

4 EXHIBITIONS 会展 5 PLANNED CONSTRUCTION 规划建设 6 SUPPORTING ENVIRONMENT 配套环境 7 CULTURE 文化

CONTENTS
目录

4 EXHIBITIONS 会展

5 PLANNED CONSTRUCTION 规划建设

6 SUPPORTING ENVIRONMENT 配套环境

7 CULTURE 文化

CONTENTS
目录

1 GENERAL INTRODUCTION OF THE ZONE 区域概览

2 FINANCE 金融发展

3 INSTITUTIONS ESTABLISHED 新设机构

 EXHIBITIONS 会展　 PLANNED CONSTRUCTION 规划建设　 SUPPORTING ENVIRONMENT 配套环境　 CULTURE 文化

1
GENERAL INTRODUCTION OF THE ZONE

区域概览

2013

LUJIAZUI FINANCIAL &
TRADE ZONE YEARBOOK
2013陆家嘴金融城年鉴
Abridged Version | 中英对照简缩版

区域概览
General Introduction of the
Zone

NO.1

The Lujiazui Finance and Trade Zone in Shanghai is China's only national-level development zone dedicated to the financial services industry and also is home to a number of other important businesses in the shipping, trade, tourism and exhibition sectors. After more than 20 years of steady development,

Lujiazui has evolved into one of the paramount hubs of commerce in Shanghai and stands as a sterling example of the city's modernization and fruits of China's economic reforms.

Lujiazui is located within the Pudong district of Shanghai's In-

ner Ring Road and spans a total of 31.78 square kilometers.

1
Photographer / ORUN
摄影 /ORUN

　　陆家嘴金融贸易区是国内唯一以"金融贸易"命名的国家级开发区，是上海建设国际金融中心的重要承载区，经过 20 多年的开发建设，已发展成具有金融业高度集聚优势和特色，集金融、航运、贸易、商业、旅游、会展等功能于一体的现代服务业集聚区和中央商务区，是中国改革开放的标志性窗口、上海现代化建设的最精彩缩影。陆家嘴金融贸易区面积 31.78 平方公里，即上海内环线以内的浦东部分。

2013

LUJIAZUI FINANCIAL &
TRADE ZONE YEARBOOK
2013陆家嘴金融城年鉴
Abridged Version | 中英对照简缩版

区域概览
General Introduction of the
Zone

NO.1

▶ **Foreign and Chinese financial institutions:** As of the end of 2012, there were 662 licensed financial institutions in Lujiazui, an increase of 5.1% over the previous year, accounting for about 90% of the total in the Pudong district and 60% of the total in Shanghai; 18 foreign banks, accounting for 82% of the total number of banks in Shanghai and half nationally; 31 fund management companies, accounting for 86% of the total in Shanghai and 40% nationally, 35 financial leasing companies, accounting for 38% of the total in the Pudong district and 30% in Shanghai overall and 415 equity investments (including venture capital) accounting for 54% of the total in the Pudong district.

▶ 中外金融机构集聚：截至年底，陆家嘴有持牌类金融机构662家，比上年增长5.1%，约占浦东新区90%，约占上海市60%，其中外资法人银行18家，约占上海市的82%，约占全国的一半；基金管理公司31家，约占上海市的86%，全国的40%。融资租赁公司35家，约占浦东新区的38%、上海市的30%。股权投资公司（含创业投资）415家，约占浦东新区的54%。

▶ **Multinational company headquarters:** As of the end of 2012, there were 81 Asia-Pacific regional headquarters of multinational companies in Lujiazui, accounting for 42 percent of the total in the Pudong district. They included 12 corporate regional headquarters, two corporate headquarters of domestic companies and 2 operations centers.

▶ 跨国公司总部集聚：截至年底，累计引进跨国公司地区总部81家，约占浦东新区42%。完成12家企业的区域性总部、2家国内大企业总部、2家营运中心的认定。

1
Photographer / Liu Bingbiao
摄影 / 刘炳标

2
Provided by IC Press
供图 /IC Press

▶ **Factor markets:** securities, futures, diamonds, oil, financial futures, talent, agricultural products, chemicals and 11 other national and municipal markets.

▶ 要素市场集聚：拥有证券、期货、钻石、石油、金融期货、人才、农产品、化工等11家国家级和市级要素市场。

3 **4**
Provided by ORUN
供图 /ORUN

2013

LUJIAZUI FINANCIAL &
TRADE ZONE YEARBOOK
2013 陆家嘴金融城年鉴
Abridged Version | 中英对照简缩版

区域概览
General Introduction of the
Zone

NO.1

▶ **Shipping firms:** As of the end of 2012, there were a total of 890 shipping firms and other companies involved in the shipping sector. Foreign investment accounted for ¼ of the overall investment in the shipping sector. 14 companies in Lujiazui identified shipping as the main focus of their business, accounting for 30% of the overall number of such firms in the Pudong district.

▶ **航运机构集聚：**截至年底，陆家嘴航运及相关服务机构 890 家。境外投资航运机构数约占区域航运企业总数的 1/4。认定重点航运企业 14 家，占浦东新区约 30%。

▶ **Commercial office buildings:** As of the end of 2012, there were 31 regional projects under construction, with a total ground floor area of 2.93 million square meters. Of the 7 projects that were completed, the ground floor area was 350,000 square meters. Of the 9 projects under construction, the total investment was 18.8 billion yuan and the ground floor area 940,000 square meters. There are an additional ten key projects including the Shanghai Tower and Shanghai International Financial Center with a total construction area of 2,440,000 square meters.

▶ **商办楼宇高度集聚：**截至年底，区域在建项目 31 项，地上建筑面积 293 万平方米。7 个项目竣工，地上建筑面积 35 万平方米。9 个项目开工建设，总投资 188 亿元，地上建筑面积 94 万平方米。确定上海中心大厦、上海国际金融中心等十大项目为2012年十大重点工程，地上总建筑面积约 244 万平方米。

2

▶ **Talent recruitment:** Within Lujiazui's core area of "two centers," 410,000 professionals are working, among them 160,000 financial professionals.

▶ **人才集聚：**陆家嘴作为"两个中心"建设核心区正发挥着巨大的吸引力，区域人才总量 41 万，金融从业人员 16 万。

1

3

▶ **Commercial facilities:** There are many world-class commercial facilities in Lujiazui, notably high-end shopping malls featuring the flagship stores of luxury brands in China. These facilities include the Shanghai IFC, Super Brand Mall, Shanghai Yaohan, Plaza 96, the Pudong Kerry Center, Western Union Square, and the Thumb Square These outlets all feature the latest fashion and lifestyle products.

▶ **商业设施齐全**：陆家嘴金融城商业设施齐全且分布合理，区域内高档商场和旗舰品牌齐集，商业设施一流，氛围浓厚。以国金中心商场、正大广场、第一八佰伴、96 广场、浦东嘉里城、联洋广场和大拇指广场等大型商场为主形成的商圈吸引了区域内外游客前来，一直以来"超前"地将时尚商品和最新的生活方式引荐给公众，从而最大限度地满足消费者需求。

2013

LUJIAZUI FINANCIAL &
TRADE ZONE YEARBOOK
2013陆家嘴金融城年鉴
Abridged Version | 中英对照简缩版

区域概览
General Introduction of the
Zone

NO.1

▶ **World-class residences and hotels:** Like the world's other great financial capitals the City of London, the Manhattan borough of New York City and Hong Kong, the Lujiazui Financial City offers outstanding residences for both those visiting the city and those residing long-term. Within Lujiauzi, there are now 22 officially ranked hotels that are 4 stars or higher as well as other hotels to meet the needs of different market segments.

▶ **生活设施一流：**陆家嘴金融城不仅致力于建成与伦敦金融城、纽约曼哈顿金融城和香港金融城等相媲美的金融城，同时还积极打造成"宜居福地"的幸福之城。城内各类宾馆酒店众多，目前正式挂牌的四星级以上宾馆有22家，经济连锁酒店也遍及金融城各个区域，满足不同消费群体需求。

Photographer / Yang Huanmin
摄影 / 杨焕敏

Provided by Grand Hyatt Shanghai
供图 / 上海金茂君悦大酒店

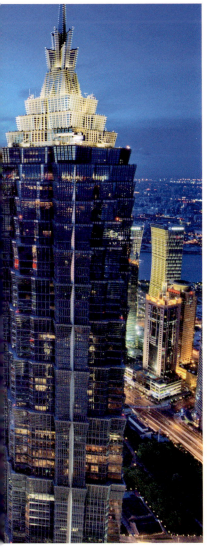

▶ **Comprehensive transportation links:** Lujiazui is an important transportation hub in Pudong that comprises an integrated network of bridges, tunnels, rail and subway lines. The Lujiazui Finance and Trade Zone is 35 kilometers away from the Pudong International Airport, 15 kilometers from Hongqiao International Airport, 20 km from the Waigaoqiao Deep-Water Port and 60 kilometers from the Yangshan Deep-Water Port.

▶ **交通便捷高效**：陆家嘴是浦东乃至上海重要的交通枢纽，跨江大桥、海底隧道、磁悬浮列车、地铁线路织成密集的交通网络。陆家嘴金融贸易区距浦东国际机场 35 公里，虹桥国际机场 15 公里，距外高桥深水港 20 公里，洋山深水港 60 公里。

▶ **Rich tourism resources:** The Lujiazui Finance and Trade Zone has many tourist attractions including the World Financial Center, Jin Mao Tower, and Oriental Pearl Tower, which receive tens of thousands of guests every day. Additionally, the 632-meter Shanghai Center will become a new landmark of the city, attracting visitors from all over the world to visit.

▶ **都市旅游资源丰富**：陆家嘴金融贸易区拥有众多旅游景点，环球金融中心、金茂大厦和东方明珠塔每日都接待着数以万计世界各地宾客，建设中的高 632 米的上海中心也将成为上海的新地标，吸引五湖四海宾客前来参观旅游。

3
Provided by Kerry Hotel Pudong
供图 / 上海浦东嘉里酒店

4
Photographer / ORUN
摄影 /ORUN

LUJIAZUI FINANCIAL &
TRADE ZONE YEARBOOK
2013陆家嘴金融城年鉴
Abridged Version | 中英对照简缩版

区域概览
General Introduction of the
Zone

NO.1

▶ **Top cultural attractions:** The Lujiazui Finance and Trade Zone has many outstanding cultural sites, such as the modern Oriental Art Center, Shanghai Science and Technology Museum, Zendai Himalayas Centre and Shanghai Jade Gallery. The city's history over the past century is depicted in the Shanghai Urban Development History Museum. Other museums include the Securities Museum, Museum of Bank of Communications, Aurora Museum and others reflecting Lujiazui's distinctive characteristics.

▶ **一流的文化设施:**陆家嘴金融贸易区有众多优秀的文化场所,不仅有充满现代感的东方艺术中心、上海科技馆、证大喜马拉雅中心、上海翡翠画廊,有作为上海近百年来发展史的史志性博物馆——上海城市历史发展陈列馆,还有历道证券博物馆、交通银行博物馆、震旦博物馆和期货博物馆等各具金融特色的博物馆,反映了陆家嘴鲜明的金融特征。

▶ **Frequent international exhibitions:** The Lujiazui Finance and Trade Zone has first-class facilities and fully functional exhibition spaces, such as the Shanghai International Convention Center, Shanghai New International Expo Centre and Pudong Expo which feature excellent hardware and software services. In 2012, 95 international exhibitions were held in Lujiazui, accounting for 35.8% of the total held in the city. Lujiazui has laid a solid foundation for the development of Shanghai's exhibition and conference industry and also provides a strong platform for exchanges between visitors from around the world.

▶ **国际会展频繁:**陆家嘴金融贸易区拥有设施一流、功能齐全的会展场所,诸如上海国际会议中心、上海新国际博览中心以及浦东展览馆等,无论在硬件设施建设还是在软件配套服务上都具备举办国际性会议、展览的条件,2012年陆家嘴金融贸易区共举办国际性展览95次,占全市的35.8%。它们不仅为陆家嘴的会展业发展奠定了坚实的基础,也为世界各地的参展商提供了一个广泛交流的良好平台,吸引着来自全国和世界各地的参展商。

1
Photographer / ORUN
摄影 /ORUN

2

FINANCE

金融发展

SHANGHAI HOLDS THIRD FINANCIAL FORUM
第三届上海金融论坛举行
CHINESE ACADEMY OF SOCIAL SCIENCES HOLDS SECOND
SHANGHAI FORUM
第二届中国社科院上海论坛举行
SILVER FUTURES CONTRACTS TRADED ON THE SHANGHAI
FUTURES EXCHANGE
白银期货合约在上海期货交易所上市交易
SHANGHAI HOLDS NINTH DERIVATIVES MARKET FORUM
第九届上海衍生品市场论坛召开
2012 CHINA EMERGING FINANCIAL DEVELOPMENT FORUM HELD IN
SHANGHAI
2012 中国新兴金融发展论坛举行
FIFTH LUJIAZUI FORUM KICKS OFF
以"金融治理改革与实体经济发展"为主题的第五届陆家嘴论坛开幕
NINTH CHINA INTERNATIONAL FINANCE FORUM HELD
第九届中国国际金融论坛举行
2012 CEO GLOBAL DEVELOPMENT CONFERENCE HELD
2012 全球 CEO 发展大会举行
......

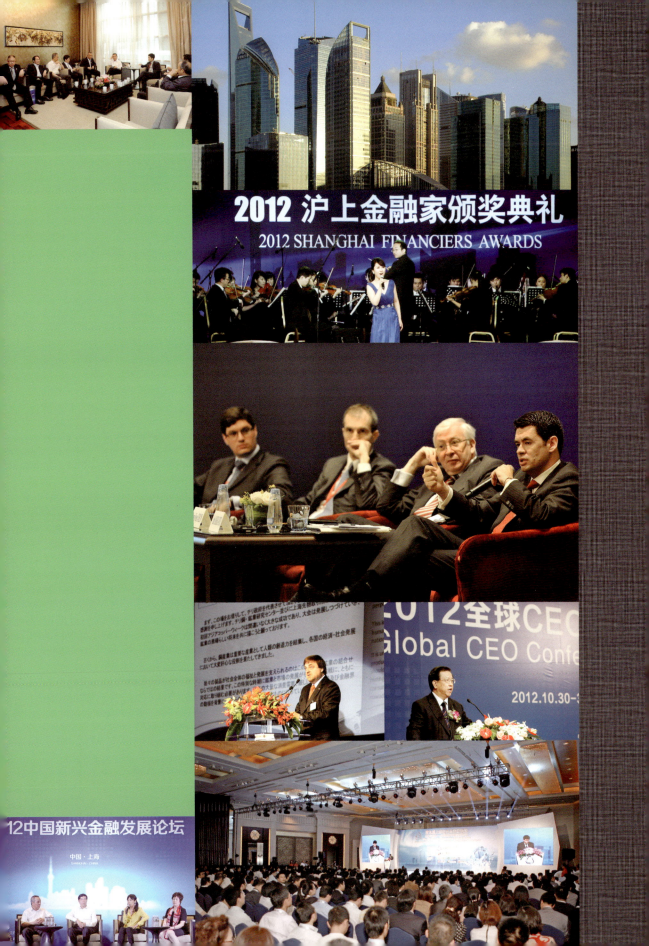

2012 沪上金融家颁奖典礼
2012 SHANGHAI FINANCIERS AWARDS

2012全球CEO
Global CEO Confe
2012.10.30-3

12中国新兴金融发展论坛
中国·上海

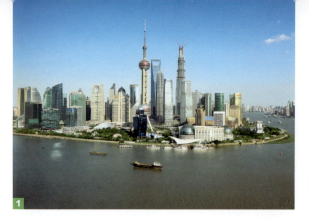

2012-1-30

NATIONAL REFORM AND DEVELOPMENT COMMISSION PUBLISHES "CONSTRUCTION PLAN OF THE SHANGHAI INTERNATIONAL FINANCIAL CENTER DURING THE PERIOD OF THE 12th FIVE-YEAR PLAN"

▶ January 30 – The National Reform and Development Commission published the "Construction Plan of the Shanghai International Financial Center During the Period of the 12th Five-Year Plan." The key themes of the plan were the internationalization of the RMB and innovation. This document follows a prior one published in 2009 by the State Council entitled " On Accelerating the Development of Shanghai's Modern Service and Advanced Manufacture Sector and Building an International Financial and Shipping Center" and is another milestone in that process.

国家发展和改革委员会公布《"十二五"时期上海国际金融中心建设规划》（摘要）

1月30日，国家发展和改革委员会公布《"十二五"时期上海国际金融中心建设规划》（下简称《规划》）（摘要）。"人民币"、"创新"以及"国际化"成为"十二五"期间上海建设国际金融中心的关键词汇。《规划》是继2009年国务院《关于推进上海加快发展现代服务业和先进制造业建设国际金融中心和国际航运中心的意见》颁布后上海国际金融中心建设进程中的又一重要里程碑。

2012-2-18

SHANGHAI HOLDS THIRD FINANCIAL FORUM

▶ February 18 – The third Shanghai Financial Forum was held at the Shanghai International Convention Center with Vice Mayor Tu Guangshao in attendance. The forum explored three major themes: "Reform of the international monetary system and the international use of the RMB," "The RMB's international use and reform of the financial system in China" and "The RMB offshore and onshore markets."

第三届上海金融论坛举行

2月18日，第三届上海金融论坛在上海国际会议中心举行。上海市委常委、副市长屠光绍出席会议并讲话。本届论坛围绕"国际货币体系改革与人民币国际使用"、"人民币国际使用与中国金融体系改革"、"人民币离岸市场与在岸市场"3大主题展开探讨。

2013

LUJIAZUI FINANCIAL &
TRADE ZONE YEARBOOK
2013陆家嘴金融城年鉴
Abridged Version | 中英对照简缩版

金融发展
FINANCE

NO.2

2

LUJIAZUI FINANCIAL & TRADE ZONE YEARBOOK
2013陆家嘴金融城年鉴
Abridged Version | 中英对照简缩版

金融发展
FINANCE

NO.2

1 2 3
Provided by Lujiazui Intitute of CASS
供图 / 中国社会科学院陆家嘴研究基地

2012-5-9

CHINESE ACADEMY OF SOCIAL SCIENCES HOLDS SECOND SHANGHAI FORUM

▶ May 9 - The Chinese Academy of Social Sciences held the second Shanghai Forum with the "Restructuring and development driven by innovation: The Shanghai example" as the theme. Politburo member and Shanghai Municipal Committee Party Secretary Han Zheng and Wang Weiguang, executive vice president of CASS both attended and delivered a speech, respectively. At the meeting, the Chinese Academy of Social Sciences Lujiazui Research Base shared a report entitled "Shanghai Restructuring and Development Studies."

第二届中国社科院上海论坛举行

　　5月9日，第二届中国社会科学院上海论坛举行。本次论坛以"创新驱动、转型发展：上海的实践"为主题。中央政治局委员，中共上海市委书记韩正、中国社会科学院常务副院长王伟光出席并致辞。会上，中国社科院陆家嘴研究基地发布了《上海转型发展研究报告》。

2012-5-10

SILVER FUTURES CONTRACTS TRADED ON THE SHANGHAI FUTURES EXCHANGE

▶ May 10 –28 types of silver futures contracts were traded on the Shanghai Futures Exchange. Liu Xinhua, vice chairman of the China Securities Regulatory Commission and Tu Guangshao, standing member of the Shanghai Municipal Committee and Vice Mayor of Shanghai, jointly inaugurated trading of the silver futures contracts.

白银期货合约在上海期货交易所上市交易

5月10日，白银期货合约在上海期货交易所上市交易，至此国内期货市场已上市28个期货品种。中国证监会副主席刘新华和上海市市委常委、副市长屠光绍共同为白银期货合约揭牌，并为开盘交易鸣锣。

1

Provided by Shanghai Futures Exchange
供图／上海期货交易所

2013

LUJIAZUI FINANCIAL &
TRADE ZONE YEARBOOK
2013陆家嘴金融城年鉴
Abridged Version | 中英对照简缩版

金融发展
FINANCE

NO.2

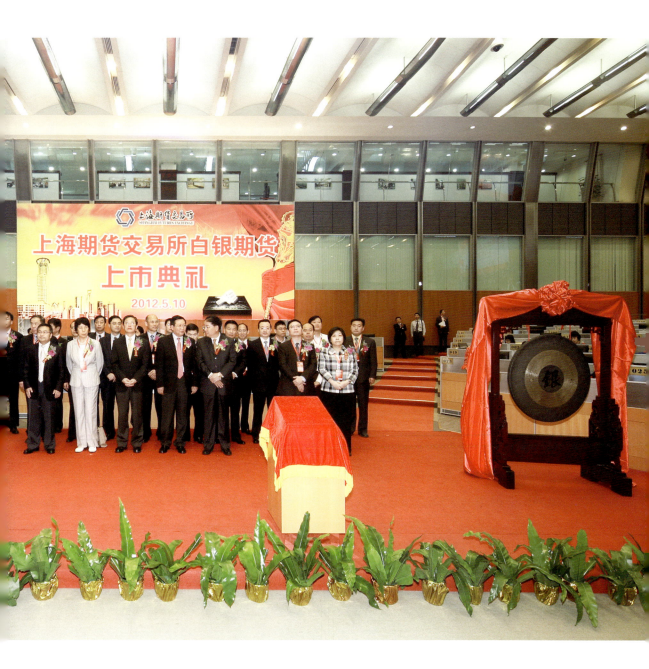

2013

LUJIAZUI FINANCIAL &
TRADE ZONE YEARBOOK
2013陆家嘴金融城年鉴
Abridged Version | 中英对照简缩版

金融发展
FINANCE

NO.2

1 2
Provided by IC Press
供图 /IC Press

3
Provided by Shanghai Futures Exchange
供图 / 上海期货交易所

2012-5-28—5-29

SHANGHAI HOLDS NINTH DERIVATIVES MARKET FORUM

▶ May 28 to 29 - The Ninth Shanghai Derivatives Market Forum was held at the Pudong Shangri-La Hotel with the theme of innovation and service in Chinese futures market reform and opening up. During the meeting, several other seminars were held, among them the International Gold Symposium, the Outstanding Figures International Forum, International Nonferrous Metal Symposium and the International Steel Symposium. The forum was hosted by the Shanghai Futures Exchange.

第九届上海衍生品市场论坛召开

　　5月28—29日，第九届上海衍生品市场论坛在浦东香格里拉大酒店召开。本届论坛的主题为创新与服务—中国期货市场的改革开放。会议期间，分别举行了黄金国际研讨会、国际杰出者论坛、有色金属国际研讨会、钢材国际研讨会。论坛由上海期货交易所主办。

2013

LUJIAZUI FINANCIAL &
TRADE ZONE YEARBOOK
2013陆家嘴金融城年鉴
Abridged Version | 中英对照简缩版

金融发展
FINANCE

NO.2

2012-6-17

2012 CHINA EMERGING FINANCIAL DEVELOPMENT FORUM HELD IN SHANGHAI

▶ June 17 – The 2012 China Emerging Financial Development Forum was jointly held in the Pudong district of Shanghai by the Chinese Academy of Social Sciences Financial Research Institute Lujiazui Research Base and the Financial Service Bureau of the Pudong New District Government. More than 200 experts from government agencies, research institutes, banks and the business community gathered at the forum to discuss challenges currently facing the financial industry, such as how to provide small enterprises with easier access to loans and financing.

2012 中国新兴金融发展论坛举行

6 月 17 日，由中国社科院金融研究所陆家嘴研究基地和浦东新区金融服务局共同主办的"2012 中国新兴金融发展论坛"在浦东举办。来自政府机构、科研院所、银行和企业界的 200 余位专家就现阶段金融业的发展环境，针对小型企业信贷、融资问题解决途径等展开讨论。

2013

LUJIAZUI FINANCIAL &
TRADE ZONE YEARBOOK
2013陆家嘴金融城年鉴
Abridged Version | 中英对照简缩版

金融发展
FINANCE

NO.2

2012-6-28

FIFTH LUJIAZUI FORUM KICKS OFF

▶ June 28 – The fifth Lujiazui Forum opened with the theme of "financial management reform and development of the real economy" at the Pudong Shangri-La Hotel. The forum featured 4 plenary sessions, 10 seminars and 8 Pujiang River Special Sessions. Topics covered included "Improving innovation in the insurance market and social security system," "Building an international financial center in Shanghai," "New shipping finance development" and "Construction and development of small and micro enterprises in accordance with the financial system." The forum was jointly organized by the Shanghai Municipal Government and the People's Bank of China, the CBRC, CSRC and CIRC. People's Bank of China Governor Zhou Xiaochuan and Shanghai Municipal Committee Party Secretary Han Zheng jointly served as co-chairs of the forum.

以"金融治理改革与实体经济发展"为主题的第五届陆家嘴论坛开幕

6月28日，以"金融治理改革与实体经济发展"为主题的第五届陆家嘴论坛在浦东香格里拉大酒店开幕。本次陆家嘴论坛共设4场全体大会、10场专题论坛、8个浦江夜话专题。涉及的主题有"保险市场创新与养老保障体制的完善"、"上海国际金融建设"、"航运金融新发展"、"构建与小微企业发展相匹配的金融体系"等。论坛由上海市政府和中国人民银行、银监会、证监会、保监会共同主办，中国人民银行行长周小川和中共上海市委书记韩正担任本次论坛联合主席。

1
Provided by IC Press
供图 /IC Press

Paths of RMB Capital Account Convertibility
人民币资本项目可兑换的路径

承办: 中国外汇交易中心
Sponsor: China Foreign Exchange Trade System

2012年6月28-30日 中国·上海
June 28-30, 2012, Shanghai, China

2013

LUJIAZUI FINANCIAL &
TRADE ZONE YEARBOOK
2013陆家嘴金融城年报
Abridged Version｜中英对照简缩版

金融发展
FINANCE

NO.2

1 **2**
Provided by IC Press
供图 /IC Press

3 **4** **5**
Photographer / ORUN
摄影 /ORUN

2013

LUJIAZUI FINANCIAL &
TRADE ZONE YEARBOOK
2013陆家嘴金融城年鉴
Abridged Version | 中英对照简缩版

金融发展
FINANCE

NO.2

2012-8-6

FORUM ON INTEGRATION OF INNOVATION AND DEVELOPMENT HELD

▶ August 6 – The Integration of Innovation and Development Forum with the theme of "The three fusions" boosting Shanghai's internationalization" was held at the Shanghai International Convention Center. The forum, which featured a number of themed lectures and interactive discussions, focused on the integration of overseas returnee and local talent, the integration of the financial and non-financial economies, harnessing the development of global finance and the construction of an international financial center in Shanghai. The forum was organized by the Shanghai Talent Work Coordination Group and Shanghai Overseas High-Level Talent Introduction Working Group.

融合创新发展—"三个融合"助推上海国际中心建设主题论坛举行

8月6日，融合创新发展—"三个融合"助推上海国际中心建设主题论坛在上海国际会议中心举行。本次论坛就重点围绕海归人才与本土人才融合、国际经验与上海国际金融中心建设融合、金融与实体经济融合3个专题开展了专题演讲和互动讨论。论坛由上海市人才工作协调小组、上海市引进海外高层次人才工作小组主办。

1
Provided by Shanghai International Convention Center
供图／上海国际会议中心

2
Provided by IC Press
供图／IC Press

2012-8-19

2012 "CAIJING FINANCIAL VALUE RANKING" LAUNCHES IN SHANGHAI

▶ August 19 – Caijing (First Financial Daily) launched "the annual First Financial Value Ranking (CFV)" Contest in Shanghai, with the theme of "Growth and reform." After a brief opening ceremony, a seminar entitled "Chinese financial reform: Seeking a new breakthrough" was held. The seminar was jointly organized by Caijing (First Financial Daily)and the Chinese Academy of Social Sciences Research Institute Lujiazui Research Base.

2012 "第一财经金融价值榜" 在沪启动评选活动

　　8月19日，由《第一财经日报》发起的"2012第一财经金融价值榜（CFV）"评选活动在上海举行，年度主题确定为"增长和改革"。在简短的启动仪式后，举行了以"中国金融改革：寻求再突破"为主题的启动研讨会。本次研讨会由《第一财经日报》和中国社科院陆家嘴研究基地共同主办。

2013

LUJIAZUI FINANCIAL &
TRADE ZONE YEARBOOK
2013陆家嘴金融城年鉴
Abridged Version | 中英对照简缩版

金融发展
FINANCE

NO.2

1 2 3

Provided by Lujiazui Finance&Trade Zone
Adimimistration of Shanghai
供图 / 陆管委

2012-10-27

FINANCIAL DEBATE COMPETITION HELD IN LUJIAZUI

▶ October 27 - 2012 The Sixth Lujiazui Financial Youth Cultural Festival Debate Finals at the Shanghai Futures Exchange ended. The current financial debate competition is divided into two major groups of financial institutions and universities. After fierce competition in the debate, the Shanghai Institute of Foreign Trade emerged victorious. The event seeks to foster a positive cultural environment for the construction of an international financial center in Shanghai as well as promote the financial culture of Pudong.

2012 年上海浦东陆家嘴金融青年辩论赛举行

　　10 月 27 日，2012 年第六届陆家嘴金融文化节暨金融青年辩论比赛总决赛在上海期货交易所落幕。本届金融辩论比赛分为金融机构组和高校两大组。经过激烈角逐，上海对外贸易学院获得本届陆家嘴金融文化节暨金融青年辩论比赛总决赛的冠军。本届金融青年辩论比赛，旨在营造和弘扬浦东新区金融文化，为建设上海国际金融中心创造良好的文化环境。

LUJIAZUI FINANCIAL &
TRADE ZONE YEARBOOK
2013陆家嘴金融城年鉴
Abridged Version | 中英对照简缩版

金融发展
FINANCE

NO.2

Provided by IC Press
供图 /IC Press

NINTH CHINA INTERNATIONAL FINANCE FORUM HELD

▶ October 28 - The Ninth China International Finance Forum was held in the Shanghai Star River Hotel with the theme of "Financial services and the real economy." The forum explored a multitude of topics germane to China's financial-services industry including the development of the financial leasing industry, financing of and investment in listed companies, commercial banking development and innovation, opportunities of and challenges facing banking organizations and leasing business, financial services and innovation, diversification of financing needs and private financial development and the impact of the Eurozone on the future development of the Chinese economy. The forum also provided other in-depth analyses of topics concerning China's financial frontier.

第九届中国国际金融论坛举行

　　10月28日，第九届中国国际金融论坛在上海星河湾大酒店举行。本届论坛主题为：金融服务与实体经济发展。论坛就融资租赁行业发展、企业上市与投融资、商业银行发展与创新、银租合作的机遇和挑战、金融服务与创新、多元化融资需求与民间金融发展，以及欧元区的未来及对中国经济影响等话题进行深层次的剖析与讲解，对中国金融发展的前沿问题进行探讨。

2013

LUJIAZUI FINANCIAL &
TRADE ZONE YEARBOOK
2013陆家嘴金融城年鉴
Abridged Version | 中英对照简缩版

金融发展
FINANCE

NO.2

1

Provided by Shanghai International
Convention Center
供图／上海国际会议中心

2012-10-30—10-31

2012 CEO GLOBAL DEVELOPMENT CONFER-ENCE HELD

▶ October 30 -31, 2012 - The CEO Global Development Conference was held at the Shanghai International Convention Center with the theme of "Emerging economies and the world: in transition to achieve a win-win." It was attended by more than 1,500 Chinese and foreign delegates, 55 percent of whom were entrepreneurs and whose companies had a turnover of more than 100 million yuan. The conference explored "How emerging economies can strengthen cooperation to tackle the financial challenges of the post-crisis era," "Internationalization of enterprises and entrepreneurship" and other issues. The conference also featured BRICS trade and investment forums, modern service industry forums, financial industry development forums and other related topics. It was jointly organized by the United Nations Industrial Development Organization and the United Nations Global South-South Development Center.

2012 全球 CEO 发展大会举行

　　10 月 30 日—31 日，2012 全球 CEO 发展大会在上海国际会议中心举行，1500 多位中外代表与会。其中企业营业额超过亿元的中外企业家占 55%。大会以"新兴经济体与世界：在转型中实现共赢"为主题，探讨"新兴经济体如何加强合作应对后金融危机时代的挑战"、"企业的国际化与企业家精神"等问题。大会还举行了金砖国家投资贸易专题论坛、现代服务业专题论坛、金融产业发展专题论坛等。大会由联合国工业发展组织、联合国全球南南发展中心联合主办。

51

THE SECOND SINO-FOREIGN BUSINESS AND POLITICAL LEADERS SUMMIT HELD

▶ November 25, "The Second Sino-foreign business and political leaders Conference" was held at the Shanghai International Convention Center. Set in the context of the European debt crisis, the forum explored a number of important relevant topics including international financial reform, monetary policy, business management, industrial investment, the sustainable development of China's economy, and facilitating new opportunities for foreign trade and economic cooperation. In attendance at the forum were former German Chancellor Gerhard Schröder, former French President Nicolas Sarkozy, former British Prime Minister Gordon Brown, "Father of the Euro" Nobel laureate Robert Mundell, Swiss central banker Philipp Hildebrand and other global luminaries.

2013

LUJIAZUI FINANCIAL &
TRADE ZONE YEARBOOK
2013陆家嘴金融城年鉴
Abridged Version | 中英对照简缩版

金融发展
FINANCE

NO.2

第二届中外政商领袖华佗论箭举行

11月25日，"第二届中外政商领袖华佗论箭"在上海国际会议中心举行。此次论坛以欧债危机为背景，就金融改革、货币政策、企业管理、实业投资等国际热点话题展开讨论，共话后危机时代，中国经济的可持续发展，探寻中外经贸合作新契机。出席论坛的嘉宾包括德国前总理格哈德·施罗德，法国前总统尼古拉斯·萨科奇，英国前首相戈登·布朗，"欧元之父"诺贝尔经济学奖得主罗伯特·蒙代尔，瑞士央行行长菲利普·希尔德布兰德等全球政商领袖。

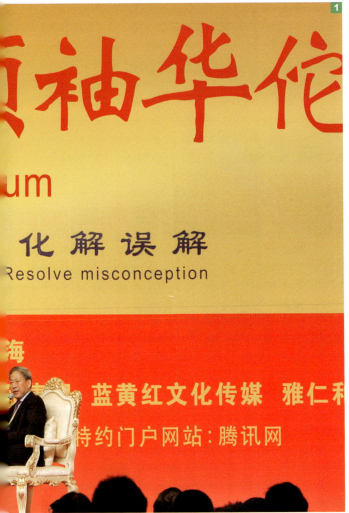

1 2 3 4

Provided by Shanghai International
Convention Center
供图／上海国际会议中心

2013

LUJIAZUI FINANCIAL &
TRADE ZONE YEARBOOK
2013陆家嘴金融城年鉴
Abridged Version | 中英对照简缩版

金融发展
FINANCE

NO.2

2012-11-28—11-29

LUJIAZUI HOLDS "THE FIRST ASIA COPPER WEEKLY CONFERENCE"

▶ November 28 -29 - The Shanghai Futures Exchange and Chile Copper Mine Research Center jointly held the first "The First Asia Copper Weekly Conference" in Lujiazui. This world-class copper industry event, the first of its kind in Asia, included a "Copper Summit," "The 8th Asian Copper Conference" and the "China International Copper and Recycling Forum" among other activities.

首届"亚洲铜周会"在陆家嘴举办

11月28日—29日，由上海期货交易所与智利铜矿研究中心共同举办的首届"亚洲铜周会"在陆家嘴举办，这是在亚洲举办的第一个世界级的铜工业领域盛会，会议包括"铜业首脑会议"、"第八届亚洲铜业大会"以及"中国国际铜加工与回收论坛"等系列活动。

1
Provided by Shanghai International
Convention Center
供图 / 上海国际会议中心

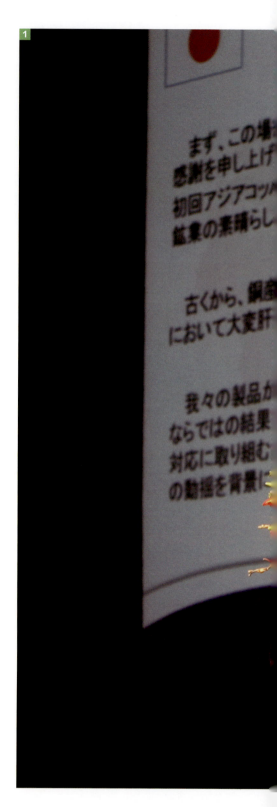

2013

LUJIAZUI FINANCIAL &
TRADE ZONE YEARBOOK
2013 陆家嘴金融城年鉴
Abridged Version | 中英对照简缩版

金融发展
FINANCE

NO.2

1 2

Provided by Shanghai Pudong New Area Shipping
Development&Promotion Center
供图 / 上海市浦东新区航运发展促进中心

SHIPPING FORUM HELD IN LUJIAZUI

▶ December 12 - The International Shipping Association Talent Forum was held in Lujiazui. Attendees at the forum included eminent shipping agencies, businesses, industry experts and academics. A total of more than 140 people gathered to discuss how to bulwark the domestic shipping industry's talent pool in the context of the global downturn in the shipping industry and other market trends. At the meeting, the Pudong New District Shipping Bureau introduced new local policies to support the industry. The event was co-organized by the Pudong New Area and the Royal Institute of Chartered Shipbrokers (ICS).

2012 国际航运人才恳谈会在陆家嘴举行

　　12月12日，2012国际航运人才恳谈会在陆家嘴举行。世界知名航运机构、企业、专家、学者等140余人齐聚恳谈会，就国内航运人才体系的完善与促进、高端航运人才的培养与引进、国际航运市场持续低迷以及后续发展趋势等话题进行探讨。会上，浦东新区航运办介绍了浦东新区航运产业扶持政策、航运人才扶持政策及浦东新区航运人才体系建设情况，英国皇家特许船舶经纪协会发表演讲，共同为上海国际航运中心建设献计献策。会议由浦东新区和英国皇家特许船舶经纪协会（ICS）共同主办。

1 2
Provided by IC Press
供图 /IC Press

58

LUJIAZUI FINANCIAL &
TRADE ZONE YEARBOOK
2013陆家嘴金融城年鉴
Abridged Version | 中英对照简缩版

金融发展
FINANCE

NO.2

2012-12-28

2012 SHANGHAI FINANCIER ASSESS-MENT RESULTS ANNOUNCED

▶ December 28, 2012 - The Shanghai financier assessment results were announced at the Pudong Shangri-La Hotel. 30 Chinese and foreign financial elites were recognized as 2012 "Shanghai Top Ten Financiers," "Shanghai Top Ten Financial Industry Leaders" and "Shanghai Top Ten Financial Innovators." Shanghai Vice Mayor Tu Guangshao , Xinhua News Agency deputy editor Shen Hai Hung and CEIBS President Zhu Xiaoming attended the ceremony. The event was jointly organized by the Shanghai bureau of Xinhua News Agency, Shanghai Headquarter of Xinhua News Agency Financial Information Platform, Caijing (First Financial) and the Shanghai Federation of Industry Finance.

2012 沪上金融家评审结果揭晓

12月28日，2012沪上金融家评审结果在浦东香格里拉大酒店揭晓，30位中外籍金融界精英分别获2012"沪上十大金融家"、2012"沪上十大金融行业领袖"、2012"沪上十大金融创新人物"奖。上海市副市长屠光绍、新华社副总编辑慎海雄、中欧国际工商学院院长朱晓明出席仪式。活动由新华社上海分社、新华社金融信息平台上海总部、第一财经、上海金融业联合会联合主办。

59

3

INSTITUTIONS ESTABLISHED

新设机构

SHANGHAI NEW INTERNATIONAL EXPO CENTER FINISHED
上海新国际博览中心全面落成
AJ SECURITIES MOVES TO LUJIAZUI FINANCIAL CITY
爱建证券有限责任公司迁入陆家嘴金融城
"XINHUA – DOW JONES MOBILE INFORMATION PUBLISHING
PLATFORM" OFFICIALLY LAUNCHED IN SHANGHAI
"新华—道琼斯移动资讯发布平台" 正式落户上海
BANK OF CHINA "SECOND HEADQUARTERS" ESTABLISHED IN
LUJIAZUI
上海期货与衍生品研究院揭牌仪式举行
NEW YORK UNIVERSITY SHANGHAI ESTABLISHED
上海纽约大学成立
SHANGHAI INTERNATIONAL SPORTS ARBITRATION COURT
HEARING CENTER ESTABLISHED
国际体育仲裁院上海听证中心成立
……

2012浦东金融人才论坛
2012 Pudong Financial Talent Forum

中国交建隆重上市
601800

完揭牌仪式

**LUJIAZUI FINANCIAL &
TRADE ZONE YEARBOOK**
2013陆家嘴金融城年鉴
Abridged Version | 中英对照简缩版

新设机构
INSTITUTIONS ESTABLISHED

NO.3

2012-1-7

ASTON MARTIN'S LARGEST GLOBAL FLAGSHIP STORE OPENS IN SHANGHAI

▶ January 7 – Aston Martin Shanghai held the opening ceremony for the launch of its global flagship store in Lujiazui. The store was located in on 266 Yangyuan Road in the Pudong district, adjacent to the Shanghai Oriental Art Center, Pudong New Area Government Hall and Century Park Park. Up to 20 show cars can be placed in its 3,600 square meter showroom. Aston Martin UK Global CEO Ulrich Bez, COO Michael van der Sande, and Asia-Pacific director Matthew James Bennett spoke at the opening ceremony, emphasizing Aston Martin's confidence in its prospects in the China market.

阿斯顿·马丁全球最大旗舰店在上海开业

　　1月7日,阿斯顿马丁上海全球旗舰店开业盛典在陆家嘴举行。开业的上海旗舰店,位于浦东新区杨源路266号,与上海东方艺术中心、浦东新区政府大厅和世纪公园毗邻。其总体营业面积约3600平方米,最多可摆放20辆展车。来自英国阿斯顿马丁全球首席执行官UlrichBez,首席运营官MichaelvanderSande,以及亚太区总监MatthewJamesBennett均出席了开业盛典并现场致辞,展现出阿斯顿马丁全面进军中国市场的信心与实力。

1

1
Photographer / ORUN
摄影 /ORUN

2013

LUJIAZUI FINANCIAL &
TRADE ZONE YEARBOOK
2013陆家嘴金融城年鉴
Abridged Version | 中英对照简缩版

新设机构
INSTITUTIONS ESTABLISHED

NO.3

2012-2-15

SHANGHAI NEW INTERNATIONAL EXPO CENTER FINISHED

▶ February 15 - The Shanghai New International Expo Center was completed. The project is jointly invested by Shanghai Lujiazui Exhibition Development Co., Ltd. and the German International Exhibition Group. Construction officially began in Shanghai Finance and Trade Zone on November 4, 1999 and was expanded after 12 times of extention with a total investment of 4.4 billion yuan. The Shanghai New International Expo Center hosts about 80 exhibitions a year, attracting approximately 400 million visitors from China and overseas.

上海新国际博览中心全面落成

2月15日，上海新国际博览中心全面落成，项目由上海陆家嘴展览发展有限公司与德国展览集团国际有限公司联合投资建造。上海新国际博览中心于1999年11月4日在陆家嘴金融贸易区正式启动建设，历经12期扩建，总投资逾44亿元。上海新国际博览中心每年举办约80场展览会，吸引约400余万名海内外客商。

AJ SECURITIES MOVES TO LUJIAZUI FINANCIAL CITY

▶ February 16 - AJ Securities Co., Ltd. moved to the Lujiazui Financial City. The company was established in 2002 after receiving approval from the China Securities Regulatory Commission, and in October 2006 completed its capital and shares increase. By the end of 2006, it had registered capital of 1.1 billion yuan.

爱建证券有限责任公司迁入陆家嘴金融城

2月16日，爱建证券有限责任公司迁入陆家嘴金融城。该公司于2002年经中国证券监督管理委员会批准成立，并于2006年10月完成增资扩股，截至年底注册资本为11亿元。

2013

LUJIAZUI FINANCIAL &
TRADE ZONE YEARBOOK
2013陆家嘴金融城年鉴
Abridged Version | 中英对照简缩版

新设机构
INSTITUTIONS ESTABLISHED

NO.3

1 2
Photographer / Yao Jianliang
摄影 / 姚建良

2013

LUJIAZUI FINANCIAL &
TRADE ZONE YEARBOOK
2013陆家嘴金融城年鉴
Abridged Version | 中英对照简缩版

新设机构
INSTITUTIONS ESTABLISHED

NO.3

2012-2-28

"XINHUA – DOW JONES MOBILE INFORMATION PUBLISHING PLATFORM" OFFICIALLY LAUNCHED IN SHANGHAI

▶ February 28, The Xinhua News Agency Shanghai Bureau, Economic Observer Newspaper and Dow Jones & Company together launched the "Xinhua – Dow Jones Mobile Information Publishing Platform" in Shanghai. The platform will rely on Xinhua News Agency and Dow Jones Financial Information's news networks and use mobile technology to provide financial information services to financial institutions in Shanghai, boosting the construction of the Shanghai international financial center.

"新华—道琼斯移动资讯发布平台"正式落户上海

2月28日，由新华社上海分社、经济参考报社和道琼斯公司共同打造的"新华—道琼斯移动资讯发布平台"正式落户上海。发布平台将依托新华社和道琼斯的金融资讯采编网络，利用移动新媒体技术，为上海金融机构提供金融信息服务，助力上海国际金融中心建设。

2013

LUJIAZUI FINANCIAL &
TRADE ZONE YEARBOOK
2013陆家嘴金融城年鉴
Abridged Version | 中英对照简缩版

新设机构
INSTITUTIONS ESTABLISHED

NO.3

2012-3-9

CHINA COMMUNICATIONS CONSTRUCTION COMPANY LIMITED LISTED ON THE SHANGHAI STOCK EXCHANGE

▶ March 9 - China Communications Construction Company Limited, sponsored by BOCI Securities Limited, was listed on the Shanghai Stock Exchange. BOCI Securities Limited was also one of the main underwriters for this listing. This project was the most elaborate and innovative in China capital market history. China Communications Construction Company Limited was the first company that merged with its subsidiary that was listed on the A share market and also raised public funds. Lastly, China Communications Construction Company Limited returned to the A share market from the H share market. From 2007, China Communications Construction Company Limited was also the first non-financial company that employed the strategic placement mechanism of selling its shares. Previously, the Agricultural Bank of China and China Everbright Bank did also.

中国交通建设股份有限公司在上海证券交易所挂牌上市

　　3月9日，由中银国际证券担任联合保荐机构和联席主承销商的中国交通建设股份有限公司在上海证券交易所挂牌上市。该项目是中国资本市场上交易结构最为复杂的创新方案，是首家吸收合并旗下A股上市公司并向社会公众股东募集资金的H股上市公司回归A股的案例，也是2007年暂停战略配售以来，除农业银行、光大银行以外首家非金融类企业IPO采用战略配售机制的案例。

1
Provided by Guotai Junan Securities Co., Ltd.
供图 / 国泰君安证券股份有限公司

2
Provided by BOCI Securities Co., Ltd.
供图 / 中银国际证券有限责任公司

LUJIAZUI FINANCIAL &
TRADE ZONE YEARBOOK
2013陆家嘴金融城年鉴
Abridged Version | 中英对照简缩版

新设机构
INSTITUTIONS ESTABLISHED

NO.3

2012-5-23

CCTV FINANCE SETS UP NEW STUDIO IN LUJIAZUI

▶ May 23 – CCTV Finance set up a new studio on the 33rd floor of the Mirae Asset Tower in Shanghai, becoming the latest news giant to establish an information center in Lujiazui after Phoenix and the Southern Newspaper Group.

中央电视台财经频道上海新演播室在陆家嘴启用

　　5 月 23 日，继凤凰卫视、南方报业集团等新闻巨头在浦东设上海新闻中心之后，中央电视台财经频道上海新演播室在陆家嘴启用。上海新演播室位于陆家嘴未来资产大厦 33 层。

73

ICBC AXA LIFE INSURANCE ESTABLISHED

▶ July 19, ICBC AXA Life Insurance Co., Ltd was established in the Mirae Asset Tower in Lujiazui. It is one of the first pilot companies in the insurance industry that the State Council and financial regulators approved commercial banks to hold shares in. It was jointly established by the Industrial and Commercial Bank of China (ICBC), AXA Insurance, the AXA Group and China Minmetals Corporation. ICBC holds a 60% stake in the company while the AXA Group and China Minmetals Corporation hold a 27.5% and 12.5% stake, respectively. The establishment of AXA ICBC marks ICBC's formal entry into the domestic insurance market.

工银安盛人寿保险有限公司挂牌成立

　　7 月 19 日，工银安盛人寿保险有限公司在陆家嘴未来资产大厦挂牌成立，是国务院和金融监管部门批准的商业银行入股保险业的首批试点公司之一，由中国工商银行、保险集团 AXA 安盛集团及中国五矿集团公司共同合资设立。中国工商银行持有 60% 的股权，安盛中国公司和中国五矿集团公司分别持有 27.5% 和 12.5% 的股权。工银安盛人寿的成立标志着工商银行正式进入了国内的保险业务市场。

Provided by IC Press
供图 /IC Press

2013

LUJIAZUI FINANCIAL &
TRADE ZONE YEARBOOK
2013陆家嘴金融城年鉴
Abridged Version | 中英对照简缩版

新设机构
INSTITUTIONS ESTABLISHED

NO.3

2
Provided by IC Press
供图 /IC Press

2012-7-19

SHANGHAI RONGXIU EMBROIDERY MUSEUM OPENS

▶ July 19 - The Shanghai Rongxiu Embroidery Museum opened to the public in the former Li family home. The museum will protect the rich heritage of rongxiu and serve as a vehicle to pass it on to future generations. The hundred-year-old Li family home was specially renovated to create the museum's showrooms. The museum is open to the public free of charge Monday to Friday.

上海洋泾绒绣陈列馆正式落成并免费对外开放

7月19日，作为国家级非物质文化遗产项目的上海洋泾绒绣的保护传承基地（传习所）当天起正式启用。为了保护和传承绒绣这门技艺，洋泾社区在修缮的百年老宅李氏民宅中专辟了绒绣陈列室和绒绣大师工作室，同时通过各种渠道推广和普及绒绣文化和技艺，让更多人关注民间传统文化。这一绒绣保护传承基地周一至周五免费对外开放。

2013

LUJIAZUI FINANCIAL &
TRADE ZONE YEARBOOK
2013陆家嘴金融城年鉴
Abridged Version | 中英对照简缩版

新设机构
INSTITUTIONS ESTABLISHED

NO.3

2012-9-26

SHANGHAI INSTITUTE OF FUTURES AND DERIVATIVES INAUGURATED

▶ September 26 – The Shanghai Institute of Futures and Derivatives was inaugurated at the Shanghai Futures Exchange. Li Xiaohong , China Securities Regulatory Commission for Discipline Inspection Secretary, and Yang Dinghua, Deputy Director of the Shanghai Municipal People's Congress, both attended the Institute's opening ceremony and spoke .

上海期货与衍生品研究院揭牌仪式举行

9月26日，上海期货与衍生品研究院揭牌仪式在上海期货交易所举行。中国证监会纪委书记黎晓宏、上海市人大常委会副主任杨定华出席致辞，并为研究院成立揭牌。

2013

LUJIAZUI FINANCIAL &
TRADE ZONE YEARBOOK
2013陆家嘴金融城年鉴
Abridged Version | 中英对照简缩版

新设机构
INSTITUTIONS ESTABLISHED

NO.3

Provided by IC Press
供图 /IC Press

上海纽约大学成立仪式
Opening Ceremony

2012.10.15

NEW YORK UNIVERSITY SHANGHAI ESTABLISHED

▶ October 15 – New York University Shanghai was jointly established by the East China Normal University and New York University with former president of East China Normal University Yu Lizhong as president, former Cornell University president Jeffrey Raymond as executive vice president and Professor Wang Xiaojing of Yale University as provost. 300 undergraduate students enrolled for the first semester in the fall of 2013. Shanghai Municipal Committee Party Secretary Han Zheng, Shanghai Municipal Committee Deputy Secretary Cui Yin and Pudong district Party Secretary Xu Lin attended the school's opening ceremony.

上海纽约大学成立

　　10月15日，由华东师范大学与美国纽约大学合作设立的上海纽约大学成立。华师大原校长俞立中任校长，康奈尔大学原校长杰弗里·雷蒙任常务副校长，耶鲁大学教授汪小京任教务长。上海纽约大学计划于2013年秋季招收第一届本科生300名。中共上海市委书记韩正为上海纽约大学揭牌。上海市委副书记殷一璀，上海市委常委、浦东新区区委书记徐麟出席仪式。

2013

LUJIAZUI FINANCIAL &
TRADE ZONE YEARBOOK
2013陆家嘴金融城年鉴
Abridged Version | 中英对照简缩版

新设机构
INSTITUTIONS ESTABLISHED

NO.3

2012-10-19

PUDONG INTERNATIONAL FINANCIAL TALENTS CLUB INAUGURATED

▶ October 19 - The Pudong International Financial Talents Club was inaugurated. It will serve as a forum for financial professionals and will promote international financial talents in Lujiazui as well as sustainable development. The forum is co-organized by the Shanghai Pudong Financial Services Bureau, the Lujiazui Finance and Trade Zone Management Committee and Shanghai personnel services industry associations .

浦东国际金融人才俱乐部揭牌成立

　　10 月 19 日，浦东国际金融人才俱乐部在 2012 浦东金融人才论坛上揭牌成立，以期促进陆家嘴国际金融人才的可持续发展。本次论坛由上海浦东金融服务局、陆家嘴金融贸易区管理委员会、上海人才服务行业协会等共同举办。

1
Provided by Lujiazui Finance&Trade Zone Adiministration of Shanghai
供图 / 陆管委综合处

2 3 4
Provided by Yuanshen Sports Development Center
供图 / 浦东源深体育发展中心

SHANGHAI INTERNATIONAL SPORTS ARBITRATION COURT HEARING CENTER ESTABLISHED

▶ November 12 - The International Sports Court of Arbitration for Sport Hearing Center was established and the opening ceremony of Shanghai International Legal Forum was held in the Yuanshen Sports Development Center. The International Court of Arbitration for Sports (CAS) , founded in 1984, is the most authoritative international sports community dispute settlement mechanism and its Shanghai branch is the first international sports arbitration court hearing center in Asia.

国际体育仲裁院上海听证中心成立

　　11 月 12 日，国际体育仲裁院上海听证中心揭牌仪式暨 2012 上海国际体育法制论坛在浦东源深体育发展中心举行。国际体育仲裁院（CAS）成立于 1984 年，是国际体育界最权威的解决争端的机构，上海分听证中心是国际体育仲裁院在亚洲的第一个听证中心。

4
EXHIBITIONS
会展

22th EAST CHINA IMPORT AND EXPORT FAIR
第 22 届中国华东进出口商品交易会
MAJOR SEMICONDUCTOR EXHIBITION HELD
SEMICON China2012（半导体中国）展会
CHINA INTERNATIONAL PLASTIC AND RUBBER INDUSTRY
EXHIBITION
2012 中国国际塑料橡胶工业展览会
CHINA INTERNATIONAL BICYCLE EXHIBITION
中国国际自行车展览会
2012 SHANGHAI INTERNATIONAL ROBOT EXHIBITION
2012 上海国际机器人展览会
2012 PUDONG INTERNATIONAL AUTOMOBILE EXHIBITION
2012 浦东国际汽车展览会
14th CHINA INTERNATIONAL INDUSTRY FAIR HELD
第十四届中国国际工业博览会
……

2013

LUJIAZUI FINANCIAL &
TRADE ZONE YEARBOOK
2013陆家嘴金融城年鉴
Abridged Version | 中英对照简缩版

会展
EXHIBITIONS

NO.4

2012-2-9

ZHANGJIANG EXHIBITION OPENS AT THE SHANGHAI SCIENCE AND TECHNOLOGY MUSEUM

▶ February 9 – An exhibition by the Zhangjiang National Innovation Demonstration Zone with the theme of "Innovation and the Future" opened at the Shanghai Science and Technology Museum. The exhibition included finance and science-themed exhibits of which more than 60 percent were interactive. The overall area of the exhibition was 4,250 square meters and was divided into 11 galleries. There were 179 items related to strategic emerging industries, 79 related to innovation or independent patents, 54 related to domestic advanced technology and 62 related to international advanced technology.

张江国家自主创新示范区创新成果展在上海科技馆开幕

2月9日，以"创新与未来"为主题的上海张江国家自主创新示范区创新成果展在上海科技馆开幕。成果展以"创新与未来"为主题，融成果性、科普性、互动性、趣味性为一体，面积约4250平方米，分为11个展区。战略性新兴产业的展项有179项；其中自主创新或自主专利展项79项，国内首创的先进技术展项54项，位于国际前列的新技术展项62项；可供观众互动的展项占60%以上。

1
Photographer / ORUN
摄影 /ORUN

2012 CHINA EXHIBITION LEADERS FORUM HELD

▶ February 15 to 17 – The 2012 China Exhibition Leaders Forum, themed "New Situations and New Trends" was held in the Pudong New District. More than 200 representatives from relevant departments at all levels of China's exhibition industry attended the forum. At the forum, industry experts and scholars discussed new business opportunities in China's exhibition industry as well as its future direction. The event was co-organized by China Exhibition Magazine and Shanghai New International Expo Center Limited.

2012 中国会展领袖论坛召开

2月15日—17日，以"新形势·新趋势"为主题的 2012 中国会展领袖论坛在浦东新区举办。来自各级相关部门以及中国会展业界的 200 余位代表出席了本届论坛。业内专家、学者共同就新经济形势下会展业的发展方向展开讨论，把脉中国会展行业的发展机遇。活动由中国会展杂志社主办，上海新国际博览中心有限公司协办。

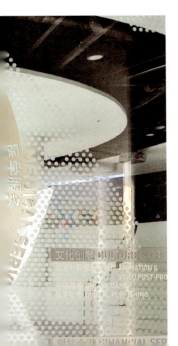

2 3
Provided by IC Press
供图 /IC Press

2013

LUJIAZUI FINANCIAL &
TRADE ZONE YEARBOOK
2013陆家嘴金融城年鉴
Abridged Version | 中英对照简缩版

会展
EXHIBITIONS

NO.4

1 2 3
Provided by ORUN
供图 /ORUN

2012-3-1—3-5

22th EAST CHINA IMPORT AND EX-PORT FAIR

▶ From March 1st-5th, the 22th East China Import and Export Fair was held at the Shanghai New International Expo Center. There were a total of 21.1 thousand participants at this year's event, an increase of 1019 people and 5.07 percent over the previous year. Businesspeople from 128 countries and regions attended the event. Export turnover totaled $3.122 billion, an increase of 9.98% over the previous year. Among them, there was $1.588 billion in textile and apparel turnover, an increase of 3.79% over 2011 and $ 1.364 billion in light manufacturing turnover, an increase of 14.34% over 2011. Private company turnover totaled $1.753 billion, increasing 34.06% over the previous year and accounting for 56.13% of total turnover. Manufacturers traded $ 2.004 billion worth of goods, an increase of 5.76% over the previous year, accounting for 64.18% of total turnover. Foreign exhibitors included 134 corporate groups, respectively, from Japan, Korea, India, Malaysia and other countries as well as Hong Kong, Taiwan and the Chinese mainland.

第 22 届中国华东进出口商品交易会

3 月 1 日—5 日，第 22 届中国华东进出口商品交易会在上海新国际博览中心举行。到会客商 2.11 万人，比上届增加 1019 人，增长 5.07%。境外客商来自 128 个国家和地区；出口总成交 31.22 亿美元，比上届增长 9.98%。其中，纺织服装成交 15.58 亿美元，增长 3.79%；轻工工艺成交 13.64 亿美元，增长 14.34%。民营企业成交占比继续上升达 17.53 亿美元，比上届增长 34.06%，占成交总额 56.13%。生产企业成交 20.04 亿美元，比上届增长 5.76%，占成交总额 64.18%。境外参展企业交易团含 134 家企业，分别来自日本、韩国、印度、马来西亚等国家及中国香港、台湾等地区，境外参展企业成交较好，促进了进出口贸易平衡。

MAJOR SEMICONDUCTOR EXHIBITION HELD

▶ March 20 to 22 – The major semiconductor industry exhibition SEMICON China 2012 was held at the Shanghai New International Expo Center, attracting the largest participation in its history. The event was approved by the Ministry of Commerce and co-organized by the China Electronic Chamber of Commerce (CECC) and Association of Semiconductor Equipment and Materials International (SEMI). The exhibition showcased the world of new technology developments and product applications, offering a comprehensive communication and collaboration platform for China's semiconductor industry. The exhibition area was divided into the following areas: LED manufacturing, IC design, manufacturing and application, TSV, used equipment and services and productivity solutions area. The event attracted nearly 1,000 exhibitors including semiconductor equipment testing manufacturers. The exhibition was held in conjunction with the Eighth China International Flat Panel Display exhibitions (FPD CHINA 2012) and China (Shanghai) International Solar Energy Technology Show (SOLARCON China 2012).

SEMICON China2012（半导体中国）展会

3月20日—22日，半导体行业最重要展会 SEMICON China 2012 在上海新国际博览中心举行。本次展会由中华人民共和国商务部批准，中国电子商会（CECC）、国际半导体设备及材料协会（SEMI）主办。展会展示了全球新技术动态和产品应用，为中国"泛半导体行业"提供一个全面沟通与协作的平台。本次展会共分 LED 制造专区，IC 设计、制造及应用专区，TSV 专区，二手设备和服务及产能解决方案专区，吸引了包括半导体检测仪器厂商在内的近千家厂商参展。同期举办的有第八届中国国际平板显示展览会（FPD CHINA2012）和中国（上海）国际太阳能技术展（SOLARCON China2012）。SEMICON China2012 的参展商数和规模达历史新高，成为全球最大的半导体展。

1
Provided by Shanghai New International Expo Center
供图／上海新国际博览中心

**LUJIAZUI FINANCIAL &
TRADE ZONE YEARBOOK**
2013陆家嘴金融城年鉴
Abridged Version | 中英对照简缩版

会展
EXHIBITIONS

NO.4

Provided by Shanghai New International Expo Center
供图 / 上海新国际博览中心

2012-4-18—4-21

CHINA INTERNATIONAL PLASTIC AND RUBBER INDUSTRY EXHIBITION

▶ April 18 to 21 - The China International Plastic and Rubber Industry Exhibition was held in the Shanghai New International Expo Center. The largest exhibition of its kind in Asia and the second-largest in the world, the event attracted about 100,000 foreign buyers, to observe and purchase the latest chemical raw materials as well as rubber and plastics machinery and technologies. The total exhibition area reached 210,000 square meters, a 17% increase over the 180,000 square-meter exhibition area over the previous year. The number of exhibitors, meanwhile, rose by 13% over the previous year, with the largest increase coming from international visitors, which surpassed the previous high and accounted for 55.2% of the overall visitors this year. Overall, 2,700 exhibitors from 35 different countries and regions were present at the exhibition, displaying more than 2,500 different machines and the latest rubber chemicals and raw materials. There were 13 exhibition pavilions: Austria, Canada, France, Germany, Italy, Japan, the United Kingdom, the United States, the Chinese mainland and Taiwan, Thailand and Korea.

2012 中国国际塑料橡胶工业展览会

　　4月18日—21日，2012中国国际塑料橡胶工业展览会在上海新国际博览中心举办。本届展会是亚洲第一、全球第二大展会，共吸引约10万名中外专业买家到场，观摩及采购最新化工原材料及各式橡塑机械及技术。展会总面积首次突破21万平方米，比上届18万平方米增长17%。展商比上届增长13%，其中国际参展商增幅最大，比上届增长高达55.2%，欧美国家参展商增加最为明显。共有来自全球35个国家超过2700家公司参展，展示超过2500台机械及最新橡塑化工及原材料。展会获得13个展团支持，包括来自奥地利、加拿大、法国、德国、意大利、日本、英国、美国等国和中国大陆及台湾地区展团，新增泰国和韩国展团。

CHINA INTERNATIONAL BICYCLE EXHIBITION

▶ April 26 to 29 – The China International Bicycle Exhibition was held in New Shanghai International Expo Center. There were more than 5,900 booths set up by 1,288 domestic and foreign companies and 120,000 square meters of indoor exhibition space. As this exhibition has become one of the pre-eminent exchange and trade platforms of its kind globally, it attracted eminent Chinese as well as European and American bicycle brands. Compared to last year, there was an increase of 50% in participation by bicycle companies from developed countries. This event was organized by the China Bicycle Association, and co-organized by Shanghai Xie Sheng Exhibition Co., Ltd.

中国国际自行车展览会

4月26日—29日，中国国际自行车展览会在上海新国际博览中心举行。本届车展共有1288家中外企业设立了5900个展位，仅室内展览规模就超过了12万平方米，成为全球展览规模最大的自行车交流及贸易平台。展会不仅云集了中国所有知名自行车企业，而且欧、美等发达国家企业参展率较去年提升50%以上。展览会由中国自行车协会主办，上海协升展览有限公司承办。

2013

LUJIAZUI FINANCIAL &
TRADE ZONE YEARBOOK
2013陆家嘴金融城年鉴
Abridged Version | 中英对照简缩版

会展
EXHIBITIONS

NO.4

2012-5-5

INTERNATIONAL RARE EGG ART EXHIBITION

▶ May 5 – The International Rare Egg Art Exhibition kicked off in Shanghai's Pudong new district at the Lujiazui IFC Mall. The works on display were done by three egg carving masters: Nan Klein, Eileen Tokita and Alan Rabon. Quail eggs, chicken eggs, goose eggs , ostrich eggs and peacock eggs were the main vehicles for the artists' work and were hand-painted, cut and polished to create their finished works. Exquisite workmanship was evident in the artists' works, especially those that were embossed, engraved or decorated with pearls and other precious stones.

国际珍稀艺术蛋展

5月5日，一场国际级的珍稀艺术蛋展亮相上海浦东陆家嘴上海国金中心商场。出自3位美国蛋雕大师南－克莱因（Nan Klein）、艾琳－托基塔（Eileen Tokita）、艾伦－拉本（Alan Rabon）之手的展品，以鹌鹑蛋、鸡蛋、鹅蛋、鸵鸟蛋和孔雀蛋等为主体，经设计、手绘、切割、雕琢等工序制作而成。艺术蛋结合浮雕、透雕的工艺，缀以珍珠宝石等珍贵材质，做工精湛，惟妙惟肖。

Provided by IC Press
供图 /IC Press

2013

LUJIAZUI FINANCIAL &
TRADE ZONE YEARBOOK
2013陆家嘴金融城年鉴
Abridged Version | 中英对照简缩版

会展
EXHIBITIONS

NO.4

1
Provided by Shanghai International Convention Center
供图 / 上海国际会议中心

2 3 4
Provided by IC Press
供图 /IC Press

2012-5-14—5-16

THIRD INTERNATIONAL VOCATIONAL AND TECHNICAL EDUCATION CONFERENCE HELD

▶ May 14 to 16 - The third International Vocational and Technical Education Conference was held by the Chinese government, organized in cooperation with UNESCO, at the Shanghai International Convention Center. The theme of the conference was "Honing skills for work and life"and focused on how to reform and develop vocational education to ensure all youth and adults obtain the necessary skills for work and life. The goals for the conference were multifold: to study current and future challenges of vocational education and the right measures to address them, to deepen the understanding of each country's vocational education system and to join hands to boost each nation's strategic vocational education plan.

第三届国际职业技术教育大会在上海国际会议中心召开

5月14日—16日，由中国政府与联合国教科文组织合作举办的第三届国际职业技术教育大会在上海国际会议中心召开。本次大会的主题是"培养工作和生活技能"，重点探讨如何改革和发展职业技术教育，以确保所有青年和成人均能获得工作和生活所需的技能。大会目标：一是深入研究当前和今后职教面临的挑战，探讨正确的应对措施；二是促进各国深化对职教的认识和交流经验；三是促进职教领域的国际合作，确定支持各国发展职业技术教育的战略方针。

2012-5-16—5-18

SIXTH INTERNATIONAL SOLAR INDUSTRY AND PHOTOVOLTAIC ENGINEERING EXHIBITION AND FORUM

▶ May 16 to 18 – The SNEC 6th International Solar Industry and Photovoltaic Exhibition and Forum–the largest event of its kind globally–was held at the New Shanghai International Expo Center. This event attracted more than 2000 companies from more than 90 countries and regions including Germany, the UK, France, Singapore and Taiwan. Total exhibition space exceeded 200,000 square meters while 200,000 professionals participated in the event, an industry record. This conference was approved by the Ministry of Science and jointly organized by 15 international associations.

第六届国际太阳能产业及光伏工程（上海）展览会暨论坛

5月16日—18日，全球规模最大的"SNEC第六届（2012）国际太阳能产业及光伏工程（上海）展览会暨论坛"在上海浦东新国际博览中心举行。共吸引德国、英国、法国、新加坡等90多个国家和中国台湾地区的光伏企业参与，参展企业2000余家，展览面积达20万平方米，约20万人次专业观众参展，创造全球光伏展会历史之最。该会由国家科技部批准，15家国际协会及组织联合主办。

第三届国际职业技术教育大会

Third International Congress on Technical and Vocational Education and Training

Troisième Congrès International sur l'Enseignement et la Formation Techniques et Professionnels

Третий Международный конгресс по техническому и профессиональному образованию и подготовке

Tercer Congreso Internacional sobre Educación y Formación Técnica y Profesional

المؤتمر الدولي الثالث بشأن التعليم والتدريب في المجال التقني والمهني

中国 上海
Shanghai, China

2012年5月13−16日
May 13-16, 2012

联合国教育、科学及文化组织
United Nations Educational, Scientific and Cultural Organization
中国联合国教科文组织全国委员会
Chinese National Commission for UNESCO

中华人民共和国教育部
Ministry of Education of the People's Republic of China
上海市人民政府
Shanghai Municipal People's Government

1

2

3

4

2013

LUJIAZUI FINANCIAL &
TRADE ZONE YEARBOOK
2013陆家嘴金融城年鉴
Abridged Version | 中英对照简缩版

会展
EXHIBITIONS

NO.4

2012-6-20—6-22

2012 ASIA MOBILE EXPO

▶ June 20 to 22 – The 2012 Asia Mobile Expo was held at the New Shanghai International Expo Center. The main participants were industry professionals, consumers, retailers and program developers. The slogan for this exhibition was "Leading the new mobile era." There were more than 200 companies at the exhibition displaying their wares, including a wide variety of products, among them games and mobile technology equipment. Participants at the event discussed opportunities and changes that would come to the mobile industry in the future. Special areas were set up at the expo for Angry Bird, virtual reality, mobile fashion and mobile games.

2012 年亚洲移动通信博览会

6 月 20 日—22 日，2012 年亚洲移动通信博览会在上海新国际博览中心举办。本届博览会的参与者主要为业内人士、专业消费者、零售商和程序开发者等。口号定为"引领新移动时代"，带领人们走进生活方式不断变化的移动互联网生活。200 多家企业在博览会上展示了商品、游戏及服务并对行业趋势、设备和技术等进行了分享，参会者就移动互联网行业未来的机遇与变革进行探讨。此次博览会为专业消费者设立了愤怒的小鸟专区、AR 增强实境专区、移动时尚专区、移动游戏地带及移动远程控制专区。

1
Provided by Shanghai New
International Expo Center
供图 / 上海新国际博览中心

2
Provided by IC Press
供图 /IC Press

2012-6-26—6-28

PHARMA AND BIOCHEMICAL INDUSTRY EXHIBITIONS HELD

▶ June 26 to 28 – The 2012 World Pharmaceutical Machinery, Packaging Equipment and Packaging Materials China Exhibition" and the "2012 World Biochemical, Analytical Instruments and Laboratory Equipment China Exhibition" were held in the Shanghai New International Expo Center. The combined space of the exhibitions was more than 30,000 square meters. More than 400 companies participated in the exhibition, including Bosch, Novasep, Morimatsu, Austar, Buchi, SKY, 3M, Matte , TianXiang , Tian Fu , Canaan , Enamel Majia , the Far East , Chu Tian , Qian Shan, Han Lin, Tung Fu Long, Guo Yao Long Li , Nano , Deere, Watertown and many others. In addition to the Chinese companies that participated, companies from Europe, Japan, Indina and South America were also present at the exhibition. The purpose of the exhibition was to create a trade platform for the pharmaceutical industry and related commercial activities.

2012 世界制药机械包装设备与材料中国展

6 月 26 日—28 日，"2012 世界制药机械、包装设备与包装材料中国展"暨"2012 世界生化、分析仪器与实验室装备中国展"在上海新国际博览中心举行，展会同期还举办了第十二届世界制药原料中国展。展出面积达 3 万平方米，参展企业有 400 余家。Bosch、Novasep、Morimatsu、Austar、Buchi、SKY、3M、亚光、天祥、天富、迦南、珐玛珈、远东、楚天、千山、翰林、东富龙、国药龙立、纳诺、迪尔、华通等国内外知名企业参展。除中国展外，更有欧洲展、日本展、印度展、南美展共 5 大系列展，全面打造一个服务于制药工业及相关领域的商贸平台。

LUJIAZUI FINANCIAL &
TRADE ZONE YEARBOOK
2013陆家嘴金融城年鉴
Abridged Version | 中英对照简缩版

会展
EXHIBITIONS

NO.4

1
Provided by IC Press
供图 /IC Press

2012-7-3

2012 SHANGHAI INTERNATIONAL ROBOT EXHIBITION

▶ July 3 - The China (Shanghai) International Robot Exhibition and China Robot Industry Promotional Conference were held in the Shanghai New International Expo Center. The total exhibition area was 20,000 square meters. The aims of this exhibition were to introduce advanced robotic technology and to help the Chinese robot industry to enter foreign markets. There were two categories of the products in the exhibition: industrial and service. The industrial robots included those for welding, arc welding, gas welding, cutting, gluing as well as robotic arms. Service robots included those for the household, cleaning, security, cooking, medical assistance, nursing, rehabilitation, entertainment and those that can operate under extreme conditions such as where there are high levels of nuclear radiation. Additionally, there were robots on display for ocean development, disaster prevention and disaster relief. The exhibition was jointly organized by the China Machinery Industry Federation and the Shanghai Dongbo Exhibition Co., Ltd.

2012 上海国际机器人展览会

7 月 3 日，2012 中国（上海）国际机器人展览会暨中国机器人产业推进大会在上海新国际博览中心举办。本次展会展览面积 2 万平方米，旨在引入世界先进的机器人技术与高端成果，促进中国机器人产业厂商开拓国内外机器人市场。展览会展品分产业机器人和服务型机器人两大类，包括产业机器人中的点焊、弧焊、气焊、切割、涂胶等各类机械臂、机械手；家务型机器人中，有清洁、警卫、烹饪等类型机器人；医疗救助型机器人则有看护、护理、康复等类型机器人；其他娱乐型机器人、极限操作机器人、海洋开发、核辐射环境、防灾、救灾等恶劣环境用机器人等也有展出。展会由中国机械工业联合会、上海东博展览有限公司共同举办。

TENTH CHINA INTERNATIONAL DIGITAL ENTERTAINMENT EXPO HELD

▶ July 25 - The Tenth China International Digital Entertainment Expo (hereinafter referred to as "China Joy") was held at the Shanghai New International Expo Center. The exhibition coincides with the tenth anniversary of China Joy. With "New Breakthroughs in a New Era" as the theme, the exhibition attracted 349 companies from more than 30 countries and regions. It featured 600 different digital game exhibitions in a total exhibition area of 70,000 square meters. It was the largest-scale event in the history of this exhibition. During the exhibition, a series of other conferences and competitions were held, including the "China Game Business Conference," "China Game Developers Conference" and "China Game Outsourcing Conference," as well as the "Cosplay Role Playing Anime Games Contest" and "Zhangjiang Cup E-sports Competition." Over the past 10 years, China Joy not only has become a showcase for China's game publishing companies and their new products at home and abroad, but also serves as an instrumental platform to discuss new industry trends, negotiate business deals and is complimentary to similar large-scale exhibitions in the U.S. and Germany. The exhibition was jointly organized by 13 entities: The Press and Publication Administration, The Ministry of Education, The Ministry of Science and Technology , The Ministry of Industry and Information Technology , The Ministry of Commerce, the State Internet Information Office , SARFT , The State Copyright Bureau , The General Administration of Sports, The Communist Youth League, The Central China Caring for the Next Generation Working Committee, The China International Trade Promotion Committee and the Shanghai Municipal Government.

第十届中国国际数码互动娱乐展览会

7月25日,第十届中国国际数码互动娱乐展览会(以下简称"China Joy")在上海新国际博览中心举办。此次展会恰逢 China Joy 十周年之际。以"开放、转型、突破,迎接新纪元"为主题的本届展会吸引了来自全球等 30 多个国家和地区的 349 家企业,携 600 余款各类游戏作品参展,展出面积约为 7 万平方米,规模创历届之最。展会期间,还举办了"中国游戏商务大会"、"中国游戏开发者大会"和"中国游戏外包大会"等专题会议,以及 Cosplay 动漫游戏角色扮演大赛、"张江杯"电子竞技大赛等一系列活动。10 年间, China Joy 不仅成为国内外游戏出版企业展示新产品、交流新经验、研讨新趋势、进行商务洽谈的重要平台,更成长为与美国 E3 展、德国科隆展齐名的国际性游戏产业盛会,亚洲同行业第一大展览会。展会由新闻出版总署、教育部、科技部、工业和信息化部、商务部、国家互联网信息办公室、广电总局、国家版权局、体育总局、共青团中央、中国关心下一代工作委员会、中国国际贸促会、上海市政府等十三个部门联合指导举办。

2013

LUJIAZUI FINANCIAL &
TRADE ZONE YEARBOOK
2013陆家嘴金融城年鉴
Abridged Version | 中英对照简缩版

会展
EXHIBITIONS

NO.4

2012-7-28—7-30

4th PUDONG AGRICULTURAL FAIR HELD

▶ July 28 to 30 – The Pudong district's 4th Agricultural Fair was held in the Yuanshen Sports Center Sports Stadium in Pudong New Area over a 3-day period. The fair featured more than 100 companies showcasing 500 types of products for sale. 55,000 people visited the fair and total sales of agricultural products reached 25.3 million yuan, an increase of 6.3% over the previous year.

2012 浦东新区第四届农产品博览会

　　7月28日—30日，2012浦东新区第四届农产品博览会在源深体育中心体育馆开展，100多家企业的500多个品种集中展示销售。3天时间内，吸引5.5万人次顾客到现场参观、购物，实现农产品销售总额2530万元，比上年增长6.3%。

1
Provided by Shanghai New International
Expo Center
供图／上海新国际博览中心

2
Photographer / ORUN
摄影／ORUN

2013

LUJIAZUI FINANCIAL &
TRADE ZONE YEARBOOK
2013陆家嘴金融城年鉴
Abridged Version | 中英对照简缩版

会展
EXHIBITIONS

NO.4

Provided by Shanghai New
International Expo Center
供图 / 上海新国际博览中心

Provided by IC Press
供图 /IC Press

2012-8-2—8-4

106th CHINA DAILY GOODS TRADE FAIR & CHINA MODERN HOME PRODUCTS EXPO

▶ August 2 to 4 – The 106th China Daily Goods Trade Fair & China Modern Home Products Expo was held at the Shanghai New International Expo Center. Total exhibition area was 92,000 square meters, with 3900 booths. 35,000 people attended the exhibition. This exhibition received official support from the China Commerce Association. The exhibition covered general merchandise and household goods, attracting tens of thousands of wholesalers, distributors, dealers and department stores and other buyers. Exhibits were dedicated to metal products, ceramics, glass and wood products, plastic products, stainless steel products, and household goods.

第 106 届中国日用百货商品交易会暨中国现代家庭用品博览会

　　8月2日—4日，第 106 届中国日用百货商品交易会暨中国现代家庭用品博览会在上海新国际博览中心举行。此次展会展览面积达 9.2 万平方米，展位 3900 个，参展观众约 3.5 万人。本次展会在中国百货商业协会的官方支持下，涵盖日用百货和家居用品，吸引数万名批发商、分销商、代理商及百货公司采购决策者等买家。展品范围包括五金制品，陶瓷、玻璃和竹木制品，塑料制品，不锈钢制品和家居用品。

2012 PUDONG INTERNATIONAL AUTOMOBILE EXHIBITION

▶ August 16 to 20 – The Pudong International Automobile Exhibition was held at the Shanghai New International Expo Center. The exhibition was jointly organized by the Shanghai Municipal People's Government, the Automotive Industry Branch of the China Council for the Promotion of International Trade, Shanghai Branch of the China Council for the Promotion of International Trade and co-organized by the Shanghai Pudong Branch of the China Council for the Promotion of International Trade and Shanghai Pudong International Exhibition Company. Cars were the focus of this exhibition. The event is held every two years to build a platform for exchanging technology and investment and to promote friendship, trade, industrial development and sales. Additionally, this event seeks to promote exchanges between local Shanghai companies and foreign companies to help develop the local automotive industry. The exhibition area totaled 60,000 square meters and it attracted nearly 30 million visitors.

2012 浦东国际汽车展览会

8月16日—20日，2012浦东国际汽车展览会在上海新国际博览中心举办。本届展览会经上海市人民政府批准，由中国国际贸易促进委员会汽车行业分会、中国国际贸易促进委员会上海市分会、中国国际贸易促进委员会上海浦东分会联合主办，由上海浦东国际展览公司承办。展会以整车展出为主，每两年举办一次，以搭建技术交流、投资合作等平台，做到以展交友、以展兴贸、以展促产、以展促销。加强上海市车企与国内外知名车企之间的交流，集聚汽车生产性企业和贸易性机构，促进汽车产业的发展。此次展出面积约6万平方米，吸引近30万观众。

2013

LUJIAZUI FINANCIAL &
TRADE ZONE YEARBOOK
2013陆家嘴金融城年鉴
Abridged Version | 中英对照简缩版

会展
EXHIBITIONS

NO.4

2012-9-4—9-6

2012 CHINA INTERNATIONAL LEATHER FAIR

▶ September 4 to 6 – The China International Leather Exhibition was held at the Shanghai New International Expo Center. The number of exhibitors increased 10% over the previous year while the total number of buyers reached 20,220, an increase of 16.25% over the previous year. Among them, there were 10,870 Chinese buyers, an increase of 20.22% over the previous year and 3583 foreign buyers, an increase of 1.69% over the previous year. Overall, there were 1,301 exhibitors from 41 countries and regions, representing the entire supply chain of the leather industry, from tanning companies to machinery and chemical manufacturers. Chinese companies accounted for 60.69% of exhibitors.

2012 中国国际皮革展

9月4日—6日，2012中国国际皮革展在上海新国际博览中心举办。参展商数量比上届增长 10%，买家总数 2.22 万人，比上届增长 16.25%。其中，中国买家 1.87 万人，比上届增长 20.22%；海外买家 3583 人，比上届增长 1.69%。展会云集 1301 家来自 41 个国家及地区的参展商参展，分别代表皮革产业自制革厂和制革机械生产商，到化学品公司和皮革贸易商的整个供应链，其中中国参展商占 60.69%。

1 2
Provided by Shanghai New International Expo Center
供图 / 上海新国际博览中心

THE 18th CHINA INTERNATIONAL FURNITURE FAIR

▶ September 11 to 15 – The 18th China International Furniture Fair was held at the Shanghai New International Expo Center. It was held in conjunction with the 18th China International Raw and Auxiliary Materials and Production Equipment Exhibition, 2012 China International Designer Works Trade Fair (September 11 -14) and 18th National Furniture Fair (September 11 -16) The four exhibitions were held in Shanghai New International Expo Centre , Shanghai World Expo Exhibition Area and International Furniture Village JSWB. The total exhibition area was 750,000 square meters. The number of exhibitors totaled 3,000 while there were 720,000 visitors, including 200,000 overseas buyers from 140 countries and regions such as France, Belgium, Italy, Spain, Portugal, Singapore, Malaysia, Indonesia, Philippines, the United States, Brazil, Australia, Britain, Ireland, the Netherlands , Denmark, Japan , South Korea, India, Thailand , Vietnam, China , Hong Kong and Taiwan. There were 170 foreign exhibitors, which was 20% more than last year, in a total exhibition area of 33,600 square meters. The exhibition was held concurrently with the Seventh China Industrial Design Week and China International Home Design Week that was co-hosted by the organizers and the Industrial Designers Society of China.

第十八届中国国际家具展览会

9月11日—15日，第十八届中国国际家具展在上海新国际博览中心举办。同期举办的有第十八届中国国际原辅材料及生产设备展览会、2012中国国际设计师作品展示交易会（9月11日—14日）以及第十八届全国家具展览会（9月11日—16日），4场展分别于上海新国际博览中心、上海世博展览馆及吉盛伟邦国际家具村举行，展会面积达75万平方米，参展企业数达3000家。展会观众达72万人次，其中海外买家20万人次，来自140个国家和地区。本届展会的海外展团包括法国、比利时、意大利Gimo大区、西班牙、葡萄牙、新加坡、马来西亚、印尼、菲律宾；海外参展国家和地区包括美国、巴西、澳大利亚、英国、爱尔兰、荷兰、丹麦、日本、韩国、印度、泰国、越南、中国香港和中国台湾。参展企业达170家，总海外参展面积3.36万平方米，比去年增长25%。展会同期举办第七届中国工业设计周暨中国国际家居设计周，由主办方与中国工业设计协会共同举办。

2013

**LUJIAZUI FINANCIAL &
TRADE ZONE YEARBOOK**
2013陆家嘴金融城服务
Abridged Version | 中英对照简缩版

会展
EXHIBITIONS

NO.4

2012-9-19—9-21

THE 8th CHINA INTERNATIONAL STATIONERY & OFFICE SUPPLIES EXHIBITION

▶ September 19 to 21 – The 8th China International Stationery & Office Supplies Exhibition was held at the Shanghai New International Expo Center. There were 631 exhibitors from total of 20 countries and regions, including Taiwan and Hong Kong, Germany, India, Korea, Malaysia, Thailand and the U.S. There were visitors from a total of 70 countries and regions, among them France, Germany, India, Spain, Singapore, Sweden, Switzerland and Hong Kong. The exhibition was organized by the China Light Industry Arts & Crafts Import and Export Chamber of Commerce and co-sponsored by Messe Frankfurt. The China International Stationery & Office Supplies Exhibition has been a stationery and office supplies industry communication and procurement platform since 2005. The exhibition has developed into the largest of its kind in the Asia-Pacific region.

第 8 届中国国际文具及办公用品展览会

9 月 19 日—21 日，第 8 届中国国际文具及办公用品展览会在上海新国际博览中心举办。此次展会有来自世界 20 个国家和地区的 631 家参展商参展，参展团包括中国台湾展团、中国香港展团、德国展团、印度展团、韩国展团、马来西亚展团、泰国展团和美国展团等 10 余个展团。吸引了来自法国、德国、印度、西班牙、新加坡、瑞典、瑞士和中国香港等 70 个国家及地区的参观商。本届展会由中国轻工工艺品进出口商会和德国法兰克福展览公司共同主办。中国国际文具及办公用品展览会自 2005 年起，一直是文具及办公用品行业业务交流及采购平台，该展会已发展为亚太地区同类型展会中规模最大的展览会。

2013

LUJIAZUI FINANCIAL &
TRADE ZONE YEARBOOK
2013陆家嘴金融城年鉴
Abridged Version | 中英对照简缩版

会展
EXHIBITIONS

NO.4

THE 12th CHINA INTERNATIONAL HARDWARE SHOW

▶ September 19 to 21 – the 12th China International Hardware Show was held in the Shanghai New International Exhibition Center. The overall exhibition area was 103,500 square meters with 2400 exhibitors, 90% of which were top hardware manufacturers. Among them, some 200 overseas exhibitors came from 20 countries and regions. The domestic exhibitors included major manufacturers like Anping and Huanghua from China's hardware stronghold Hebei province, Jinhua, Wenzhou, Pujiang and Haiyan from Zhejiang province and Shunde, Zhongshan and Xiaolan from Guangdong province. A total 46,368 people visited the exhibition, of which 4145 came from overseas. A number of the visitors were hardware dealers, building materials dealers, and import-export dealers. A number of multinational firms made purchases at the exhibition, including Wal-Mart, Carrefour, Home Depot, Kingfisher Group, Lloyd's , Leroy Merlin, Saint-Gobain, Metro etc.

第 12 届中国国际五金展

9 月 19 日—21 日，第 12 届中国国际五金展在上海新国际博览中心举行。本次展览面积 10.35 万平方米，展商 2400 家。90% 以上为一线制造商，其中 200 余家海外展商来自近 20 个国家和地区。国内展商涵盖了所有的行业主要企业参加，有中国五金产业基地河北安平、黄骅，浙江金华、温州、浦江、海盐，广东顺德、中山小榄等企业参加。在专业观众方面，有来自五金产品经销商、建材经销商、建筑工程及房地产精装项目设计师、采购商、进出口贸易商等各领域 46368 名观众参加展会，其中海外观众 4145 人。包括沃尔玛、家乐福、家得宝、翠丰集团、劳氏、乐华梅兰、圣戈班、麦德龙等来自近 90 个国家和地区的跨国零售商驻会采购。

1
Provided by Shanghai New International
Expo Center
供图 / 上海新国际博览中心

2
Provided by GL events China Co. Ltd.
供图 / 智奥会展（上海）有限公司

2012-10-3—10-6

31st CHINA SHANGHAI REAL ESTATE TRADE FAIR

▶ Ocotober 3 to 6 – The 31st China Shanghai Real Estate Trade Fair opened at the Shanghai Pudong Exhibition Hall. The fair was co-hosted by the Shanghai Real Estate Association, Shanghai Real Estate Economic Institute, Pudong New District Real Estate Industry Association. 40 property companies with over 60 new buildings attended the fair and almost 50% of the new buildings were from the Pudong New District.

2012 第三十一届中国·上海房地产展示交易会

　　10月3日—6日，由上海市房地产行业协会、上海市房产经济学会、浦东新区房地产业协会主办的 2012 第三十一届中国·上海房地产展示交易会在上海浦东展览馆举办。本次展会有参展企业 40 家，参展楼盘 60 余个，其中近一半是浦东新区的楼盘。

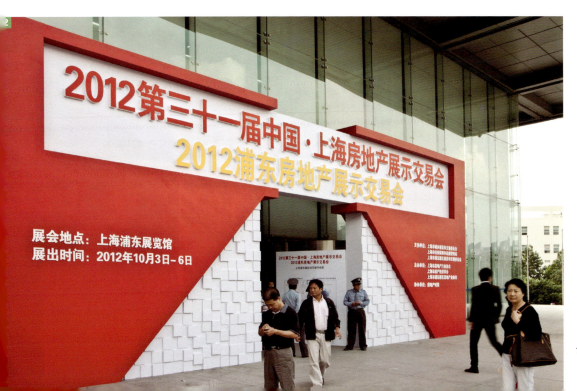

2013

LUJIAZUI FINANCIAL &
TRADE ZONE YEARBOOK
2013陆家嘴金融城年鉴
Abridged Version | 中英对照简缩版

会展
EXHIBITIONS

NO.4

1 2

Provided by IC Press
供图 /IC Press

2012-10-11—10-14

CHINA INTERNATIONAL MUSICAL INSTRUMENT EXHIBITION

▶ October 11 to 14 – The China (Shanghai) International Musical Instruments Exhibition was held in the Shanghai New International Expo Center. As the Asia-Pacific region's largest music industry exhibition, it featured a total area of 86,000 square meters, exhibitors from 30 countries and regions and 1,606 total exhibitors, an increase of 13 percent over the previous year. Additionally, there 11 regional and national pavilions, also an increase over the previous year. The exhibition brought together the Pearl, Yamaha, KHS , Peavey, Roland, Concert Music , U.S. Tegretol and other famous musical companies and brands. The exhibition was jointly organized by the China Musical Instrument Association, Shanghai International Exhibition Center Co., Ltd. and Messe Frankfurt (HK).

2012 中国（上海）国际乐器展览会

10 月 11 日—14 日，2012 中国（上海）国际乐器展览会在上海新国际博览中心举办。作为亚太地区最大的音乐产业展，本届展会规模增至 86000 平方米，共有来自 30 个国家和地区的 1606 家企业参展，展商数比上年增长了 13%，其中国家和地区展团增至 11 个。展会汇聚了珠江、雅马哈、超拨、功学社、Peavey、乐兰、知音琴行、美得理等国内外知名乐器企业和品牌。本届展会由中国乐器协会、上海国际展览中心有限公司和法兰克福展览（香港）有限公司共同主办。

逐梦神州 畅享

—神舟九号航天员

指导单位：中共上海市科学技术

主办单位：共青团上海市委员会

承办单位：同上海科学技术

支持单位：上海科技发展

2013

LUJIAZUI FINANCIAL &
TRADE ZONE YEARBOOK
2013陆家嘴金融城年鉴
Abridged Version | 中英对照简缩版

会展
EXHIBITIONS

NO.4

2012-11-2

1 3
Photographer / Chen Zhimin
摄影 / 陈志民

2
Provided by Shanghai Science &
Technology Museum
供图 / 上海科技馆

CHINA MANNED SPACE RENDEZ-VOUS EXHIBITION

▶ The China Manned Space Rendez-Vous and Docking Exhibition opened on November 2 at the Shanghai Science and Technology Museum. The Shenzhou Nine astronauts attended the opening ceremony and participated in related activities. The exhibition included the return capsule from the Shenzhou Nine mission as well as components used for the docking of Shenzhou Nine and Tiangong One, 19 spacesuits worn on the mission and 105 photos.

中国首次载人交会对接航天展在上海科技馆开幕

11月2日，中国首次载人交会对接航天展在上海科技馆开幕，神舟九号航天员出席开幕式，并参加科普交流与座谈活动。展出的实物包括神舟九号返回舱、神舟九号与天宫一号对接机构部件、宇航员从太空带回的舱内宇航服等共 19 件，照片 105 幅。

2013

LUJIAZUI FINANCIAL &
TRADE ZONE YEARBOOK
2013 陆家嘴金融城年鉴
Abridged Version | 中英对照简缩版

会展
EXHIBITIONS

NO.4

2012-11-6—11-10

14th CHINA INTERNATIONAL INDUSTRY FAIR HELD

▶ November 6 to 10 – The 14th China International Industry Fair was held at the Shanghai New International Expo Centre. With the theme of "Strategies for Transformation and Innovation in Emerging Industries," the fair included 7 additional sub-exhibitions: The Metalworking and CNC Machine Tool Show, Industrial Automation Show, Energy Show, New Energy Auto Show, Environmental Protection Technology & Equipment Show, Information & Communication Technology Show and Science & Technology Innovation Show. The display area totaled 140,000 square meters and featured 1648 exhibitors, among which there were 419 foreign companies, making up 25.4% of the overall participating companies.

第十四届中国国际工业博览会

11月6日—10日，第十四届中国国际工业博览会（简称"工博会"）在上海新国际博览中心举办。本届工博会以"创新转型与战略性新兴产业"为主题，设置了数控机床与金属加工展、工业自动化展、新能源与电力电工展、新能源汽车展、环保技术与设备展、信息与通信技术应用展、科技创新展等7个专业展，展览面积达14万平方米，有1648家国内外企业参展，其中境外企业419家，占25.4%。

113

2013

LUJIAZUI FINANCIAL &
TRADE ZONE YEARBOOK
2013陆家嘴金融城年鉴
Abridged Version | 中英对照简缩版

会展
EXHIBITIONS

NO.4

1 2 3
Photographer / ORUN
摄影 /ORUN

2012-11-11—2013-1-10

MARINE WIZARD-- PLASTICIZED SPECIMENS OF MARINE VERTEBRATES EXHIBITION

▶ Nov.11,2012 to Jan.10,2013: The Plasticized Specimens of Marine Vertebrates Exhibition was held in the Shanghai Science and Technology Museum. The exhibition was organized by the Shanghai Science and Technology Museum and supported by Shanghai Science Education Development Foundation. During the show, it was the first time the Shanghai Science and Technology Museum presented to visitors the world's most advanced biological specimen plasticizing technology. A number of deep-sea dwellers–all vertebrates–were presented, including sea bats, manta rays and whale sharks during the two-month exhibition. Attendees at the show could observe clearly the skins and decipher the interior structure of the sea animals. The visitors could also understand the survival ability of sea animals has evolved over tens of thousands of years. Overall, the exhibition made visitors more aware of the rich ecosystem supported by the ocean and the importance of preserving it.

海洋精灵——海洋脊椎动物塑化标本展

2012 年 11 月 11 日—2013 年 1 月 10 日，海洋精灵——海洋脊椎动物塑化标本展在上海科技馆开幕。本次展览由上海科技馆主办，上海科普教育发展基金会协办，是上海科技馆首次将国际上最先进的生物标本塑化保存技术呈现在公众面前的临时展览。展览历时 2 个月，展示了大量生活在海洋深处、海洋脊椎动物，包括海中蝙蝠——双吻前口蝠鲼、体型最大的鱼——鲸鲨等 70 余件塑化标本。观众通过展览，可以看到海洋生物的外观，清晰地辨认其内部结构，发现海洋脊椎动物千万年来在环境变化下演变出的各项"生存本领"，激发对海洋生命的热爱之情、关爱之意与珍爱之心。

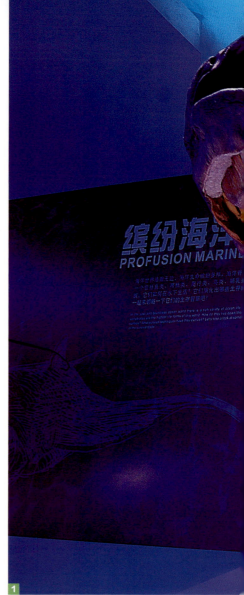

LUJIAZUI FINANCIAL &
TRADE ZONE YEARBOOK
2013陆家嘴金融城年鉴
Abridged Version | 中英对照简缩版

会展
EXHIBITIONS

NO.4

2012-11-27—11-30

BAUMA CHINA

▶ Bauma China, The 6th International Trade Fair for Construction Machinery, Building Material Machines, Construction Vehicles and Equipment, was held from November 27 to 30 in the Shanghai New International Expo Centre. As the most significant industry gathering in Asia, Bauma China 2012 for the first time covered the whole exhibition area of 300,000 square meters, including all the indoor and outdoor areas, which was a 30% increase compared to Bauma China 2010. Bauma China 2012 attracted 2,718 exhibitors from 38 countries and regions (Bauma China 2010: 1,858 exhibitors from 37 countries and regions), which was an increase of 46%. China ranked first with 1,837 exhibitors, followed by Germany (172 exhibitors), Italy (122 exhibitors), the U.S.A. (116 exhibitors), South Korea (67 exhibitors) and Japan (49 exhibitors). Among them, the joint pavilion organized by the Incheon Chamber of Commerce of South Korea attended the exhibition for the first time. Bauma China 2012 attracted about 180,000 visitors coming for business, a 16% increase compared to the last show.

中国国际工程机械、建材机械、工程车辆及设备博览会

11月27日—30日，中国国际工程机械、建材机械、工程车辆及设备博览会（bauma China）在上海新国际博览中心举办。作为亚洲最大最重要的行业盛会，2012年是bauma China首次使用上海新国际博览中心室内外全馆，展示面积共30万平方米，比2010年增长逾30%。本届展会共有来自38个国家和地区的2718家参展企业（bauma China2010：1858家来自37个国家），增幅达46%。本次展会中国以1837家参展商数量位列第一。除中国外，来自德国（172家）、意大利（122家）、美国（116家）、韩国（67家）和日本（49家）的参展企业数排名分列前5位。其中由韩国仁川商会组织的联合参展团首次参展。展会吸引了约18万名观众参观洽谈，比上届展会增加16%。

1
Provided by Shanghai New International Expo Center
供图 / 上海新国际博览中心

2 3
Provided by IC Press
供图 /IC Press

5

PLANNED CONSTRUCTION
规划建设

ORIENTAL FINANCIAL PLAZA PROJECT COMPLETED
世纪大道中段一甲级办公楼——东方金融广场工程竣工
LUJIAZUI FINANCIAL CITY TO PROMOTE 10 KEY PROJECTS
陆家嘴金融城十大重点工程建设推进会举行
MAIN STRUCTURE OF CHINA FINANCIAL INFORMATION
BUILDING COMPLETED
中国金融信息中心主体结构竣工
CONSTRUCTION STARTED ON FINAL SEGMENT OF LUJIAZUI
FINANCIAL CITY PEDESTRIAN WALKWAY
陆家嘴金融城二层步行连廊世纪连廊段工程开工
FINANCE PLAZA PROJECT KICKS OFF IN PUDONG
浦东金融广场项目开工建设
CONSTRUCTION BEGINS ON NEW YORK UNIVERSITY IN
SHANGHAI
上海纽约大学主楼钢结构工程封顶
LUJIAZUI FINANCIAL CITY UNDERGROUND PROJECT
LAUNCHES
陆家嘴金融城地下空间开发项目正式开工
......

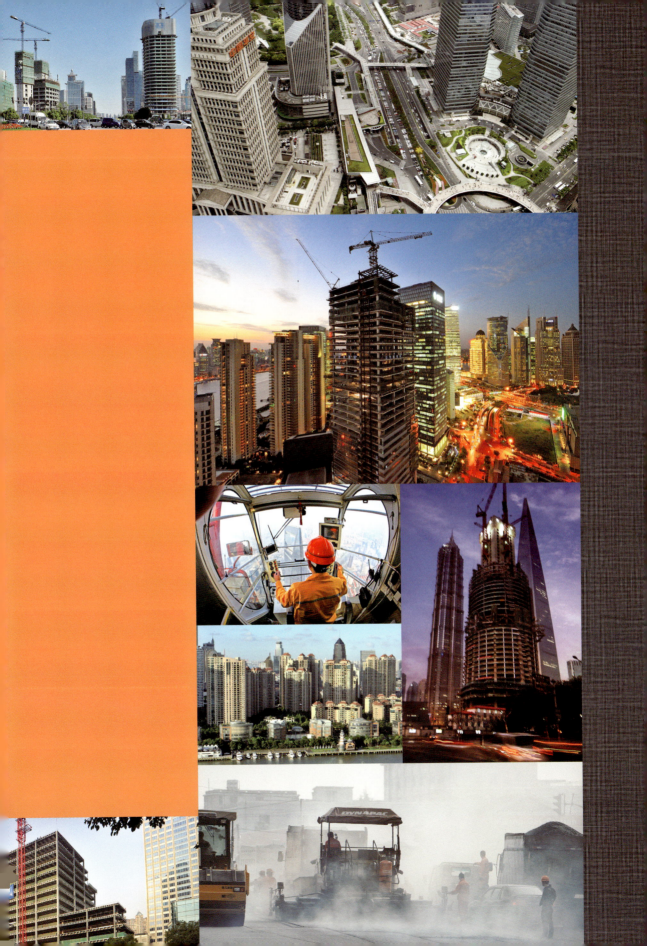

2013

LUJIAZUI FINANCIAL &
TRADE ZONE YEARBOOK
2013陆家嘴金融城年鉴
Abridged Version | 中英对照简缩版

规划建设
PLANNED CONSTRUCTION

NO.5

1
Photographer / ORUN
摄影 /ORUN

2 **3**
Provided by IC Press
供图 /IC Press

2012-3

ORIENTAL FINANCIAL PLAZA PROJECT COMPLETED

▶ The Oriental Financial Plaza project that began in July 2008 was completed in March 2012. It is located in the Lujiazui Finance and Trade Zone on 2 plots in the 2-1-1 district at the intersection of Century Avenue, Laoshan Road and Zhangyang Road. The project covers a total ground-floor area of 12,000 square meters and 94,000 square meters including all of the architecture. The project includes two office towers, one 18-story tower and one 23-story tower, and a 3-story shopping center. Total investment in the project is 2.03 billion yuan and split between Shanghai Oriental Financial Plaza and Jinhui Industrial Enterprise Development Co., Ltd.

世纪大道中段一甲级办公楼——东方金融广场工程竣工

　　东方金融广场于 2008 年 7 月开工建设，于 2012 年 3 月竣工。项目位于陆家嘴金融贸易区 2-1-1、2 地块，由世纪大道、崂山路、及张扬路围合而成，占地面积 1.2 万平方米，地上总建筑面积约 9.4 万平方米，由两幢分别为 23 层、18 层办公楼和 3 层商业裙房组成。项目总投资 20.3 亿元，由上海东方金融广场企业发展有限公司和金辉工业房地产发展公司联合投资建设。

2

1

FOXCONN'S NEW CHINA HEADQUARTERS

▶ May 10 – Construction began on Foxconn's new China headquarters, located at on the Lujiazui Ring Road and East Park junction. The building will be 95 meters high, with 21 above-ground stories and 4 underground floors, with a total construction area of 80,719 square meters. The building is expected to be completed by 2015. The building also includes Foxconn's regional headquarters in China and its research and development center in the Yangtze River Delta region.

富士康大陆新总部在陆家嘴动工

5月10日，上海富士康大厦动土，项目位于陆家嘴环路、东园路口。大厦建筑高度95米，分地上21层、地下4层，总建筑面积80719平方米，预计2015年完工。该大厦是鸿海富士康的中国地区总部，也是其在长三角地区的研发中心。

2013

**LUJIAZUI FINANCIAL &
TRADE ZONE YEARBOOK**
2013陆家嘴金融城年鉴
Abridged Version | 中英对照简缩版

规划建设
PLANNED CONSTRUCTION

NO.5

2012-5-14

LUJIAZUI FINANCIAL CITY TO PROMOTE 10 KEY PROJECTS

▶ May 14 – The Lujiazui Financial City will promote ten key projects in Lujiazui. As of the end of April 2012, the number of commercial office buildings in Lujiazui Finance and Trade Zone totaled 207, with a construction area of about 10,150,000 square meters. During the period of the 12th Five-Year Plan, Lujiazui will implement the "Expand the City" strategy and build 45 new office towers with a ground floor area of 3.5 million square meters with a total investment of about 52 billion yuan. The ten projects are comprised of the Shanghai Tower, Lujiazui Riverside Financial City Building, Shanghai International Financial Center, Shanghai IFC, Century Metropolis, Pudong Financial Plaza (SN1 plots), Tongdong headquarters, China Financial Information Building, New York University Shanghai and Lufa Square.

陆家嘴金融城十大重点工程建设推进会举行

　　5月14日，陆家嘴金融城十大重点工程建设推进会在陆家嘴举行。截至2012年4月底，陆家嘴金融贸易区商办楼宇数达到207幢，建筑面积约1015万平方米。"十二五"期间，陆家嘴金融城实施"扩城"战略，计划建设商办楼宇45幢，地上建筑面积350万平方米，加速推进其中的十大重点项目，总投资约520亿元。十大重点工程分别为上海中心大厦、陆家嘴滨江金融城、上海国际金融中心、上海国金中心、世纪大都会、浦东金融广场（SN1地块）、塘东总部基地、中国金融信息大厦、上海纽约大学和路发广场。

MAIN STRUCTURE OF CHINA FINANCIAL INFORMATION BUILDING COMPLETED

▶ July 25 – The main structure of the China Financial Information Building was completed. The project is an important part of the strategic cooperation between the Xinhua News Agency and the Shanghai Municipal Government, which aims to build a robust financial information platform, boost the construction of an international financial center in Shanghai and bulwark major infrastructure projects. The project was completed in the second half of 2013. It will be a multifunctional space for publishing, research and development and data mining.

中国金融信息中心主体结构竣工

　　7月25日，中国金融信息中心主体结构竣工，土建工程全部完成。该项目是新华社和上海市政府战略合作的重要内容，是国家"核、高、基"项目新华社金融信息平台（新华08）的重要载体，也是上海国际金融中心建设的重大基础工程。工程计划于2013年下半年完成，中心将集金融信息采集、发布，数据挖掘，指数研发，金融家俱乐部等多重功能于一身。

2013

LUJIAZUI FINANCIAL &
TRADE ZONE YEARBOOK
2013陆家嘴金融城年鉴
Abridged Version | 中英对照简缩版

规划建设
PLANNED CONSTRUCTION

NO.5

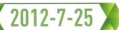

2012-7-25

SECOND PHASE OF LUJIAZUI FINANCIAL CITY RIVERSIDE PROJECT LAUNCHED

▶ July 25 – The second phase of the Lujiazui Financial City Riverside Project was launched at the Lujiazui Financial City Riverside 2E5-1 block. The project is located in the Shanghai Shipyard in the Pudong district and covers about 250,000 square meters. The ground-floor area totals 850,000 square meters, while the underground construction area is about 520,000 square meters. Designed, constructed and managed by one enterprise, the project is an integrated office, residential and commercial development, showcasing the designs of a world-class architectural design team. When complete, it will comprise Grade A office buildings that will be home to the headquarters of banks as well as a five-star hotel, luxury residences and a business center.

陆家嘴滨江金融城二期项目正式启动

7月25日，在陆家嘴滨江金融城 2E5-1 地块举行了二期项目工程启动仪式。陆家嘴滨江金融城即原上海船厂（浦东）区域，占地约 25 万平方米，地上建筑面积约 85 万平方米，地下建筑面积约 52 万平方米，由一家开发企业进行统一规划设计、统一开发建设及统一管理运营，由国际一流建筑设计团队共同打造。将集国际甲级办公楼、银行总部大楼、超五星级酒店、滨江豪宅、高端商业中心、精品文化演艺等为一体的综合立体城市新地标。

1 2
Photographer / ORUN
摄影 /ORUN

2013

LUJIAZUI FINANCIAL &
TRADE ZONE YEARBOOK
2013陆家嘴金融城年鉴
Abridged Version | 中英对照简缩版

规划建设
PLANNED CONSTRUCTION

NO.5

2012-8

CONSTRUCTION STARTED ON FINAL SEGMENT OF LUJIAZUI FINANCIAL CITY PEDESTRIAN WALKWAY

In August, construction began on the final segment of the 2-level Lujiazui Financial City Pedestrian Footbridge. The footbridge, which spans a total length of 543 meters, is located south of the Century Avenue sidewalk and west of the Yincheng Middle Road International Finance Center. It crosses Dongtai Road and is east of the World Financial Center Greenbelt. The total wideness of the footbridge is 10 meters while the net wideness of the walkway is 9 meters with the distance between the footbridge and the road no less than 5.5 meters. The footbridge is equipped with 2 escalators, 1 vertical lifts and one stairway. As of the end of 2012, the project was 85% complete.

陆家嘴金融城二层步行连廊世纪连廊段工程开工

8月，陆家嘴金融城二层步行连廊一期最后一个标段世纪连廊段开工建设。该项目位于世纪大道南侧人行道，全长543米，西起银城中路国金中心，跨越东泰路，至环球金融中心，与建设中的环球金融中心东侧绿地接通。天桥总宽10米，桥面净宽9米，跨路段桥下净空不小于5.5米，并于银城中路东侧金茂绿地、东泰路西侧、东泰路东侧各设置2台自动扶梯、1台垂直电梯和1台人行钢梯。至2012年底，该工程已完成全部桩基工程及85%的钢梁架设。

1
Photographer / Wei Shile
摄影 / 魏诗乐

2
Photographer / Yang Huanmin
摄影 / 杨焕敏

1

Provided by Lujiazui Finance&Trade Zone Administration of Shanghai

供图 / 陆管委规建处

2

Photographer / Yao Jianliang

摄影 / 姚建良

2012-8-7

FINANCE PLAZA PROJECT KICKS OFF IN PUDONG

▶ August 7 – The Pudong Financial Plaza (SN1 base) held a groundbreaking ceremony at the project construction site. Shanghai Municipal Committee Member and Vice Mayor Tu Guangshao, Shanghai Municipal Committee Member and Pudong District Party Secretary Xu Lin and Shanghai Chinese People's Political Consultative Conference Vice Chairman and Pudong New District Chairman Jiang Liang attended the ceremony. The project comprises three Grade-A office buildings, a shopping center and a 4-level underground parking garage. The total area of the office buildings is 180,000 square meters, the shopping center 120,000 square meters and the parking garage 150,000 square meters. The project is expected to be complete in 2018. The Lujiazui Company is the main investor in the project.

浦东金融广场项目开工建设

8月7日，浦东金融广场项目（SN1基地）举行开工仪式。正式开工，并于工地现场举行项目仪式。上海市委常委、副市长屠光绍，上海市委常委、浦东新区区委书记徐麟，上海市政协副主席、浦东新区区长姜樑出席仪式。项目由3栋甲级办公楼、1座商业购物中心和1个四层的地下车库组成。其中，办公面积约18万平方米，商业面积约12万平方米，车库面积约15万平方米。项目预计在2018年前竣工交付。项目由陆家嘴公司投资建设。

2012-12-7

CONSTRUCTION BEGINS ON NEW YORK UNIVERSITY IN SHANGHAI

▶ December 7 – Construction of the steel skeleton of the main New York University in Shanghai building began. The main building is 15 stories high and has a 6-story annex. Total construction area of the 2 buildings is 65,000 square meters. The school is surrounded by an attractive green belt. The school's first semester was the fall of 2013 in which 300 undergraduate students enrolled.

上海纽约大学主楼钢结构工程封顶

12月7日，上海纽约大学主楼钢结构工程封顶。该校由一栋15层主楼和一栋6层附楼组成，总建筑面积6.5万平方米，学校四周不设围墙，只有花园和绿地。上海纽约大学计划于2013年秋季招收第一届本科生300名，2014年投入使用。

LUJIAZUI FINANCIAL &
TRADE ZONE YEARBOOK
2013陆家嘴金融城年鉴
Abridged Version | 中英对照简缩版

规划建设
PLANNED CONSTRUCTION

NO.5

2013

LUJIAZUI FINANCIAL &
TRADE ZONE YEARBOOK
2013陆家嘴金融城年鉴
Abridged Version | 中英对照简缩版

规划建设
PLANNED CONSTRUCTION

NO.5

1
Photographer / Yang Huanmin
摄影 / 杨焕敏

2012-12-27

90 STORIES OF THE SHANGHAI TOWER COMPLETED

▶ December 27 – 90 stories of the main structure of the Shanghai Tower were completed and the structure now reaches more than 425 meters. When it is complete – the main building was scheduled to be finished in July 2013 - the Shanghai Tower will be 632 meters. The overall project is scheduled for completion in December 2014. The Shanghai Tower has been issued a certificate from the Ministry of Housing and Construction to certify it is a 3-star green building and also won the U.S. Green Building Council (USGBC) LEED Gold Pre-Certification Award. The Shanghai Tower is the first twin-tower high-rise building in China to be certified as green by two authoritative organziton.

上海中心大厦主楼核心筒钢结构完成 90 层

12 月 27 日，在建的上海中心大厦主楼核心筒钢结构完成 90 层，高度超过 425 米。上海中心大厦由上海建工集团总承包，总高度 632 米，计划 2013 年 7 月主楼结构封顶，2014 年 12 月工程全面竣工。在建的上海中心己获住房城乡建设部颁发的三星级绿色建筑设计标识证书，还获得了美国绿色建筑委员会（USGBC）颁发的 LEED 金级预认证。上海中心已成为国内第一座同时获得绿色建筑权威机构双认证的超高层建筑。

2013

LUJIAZUI FINANCIAL &
TRADE ZONE YEARBOOK
2013 陆家嘴金融城年鉴
Abridged Version | 中英对照简缩版

规划建设
PLANNED CONSTRUCTION

NO.5

1
Photographer / ORUN
摄影 /ORUN

2 **3** **4**
Photographer / Yang Huanmin
摄影 / 杨焕敏

2012-12

LUJIAZUI FINANCIAL CITY UNDERGROUND PROJECT LAUNCHES

▶ December 31 – Construction began on the Lujiazui Financial City Underground Space Development Project, which is located west of the Jinmao Tower under the Z2-1 block and comprises 7248 square meters of green space underneath. 5 underground passes link that green space with all of the surrounding area's key landmarks. Overall, the project covers 13,500 square meters, including a 12,300 square meters floor-area greenbelt and two underground levels. The project was designed primarily for pedestrians and local businesses. The project is scheduled for completion in early 2015.

陆家嘴金融城地下空间开发项目正式开工

12 月底，陆家嘴金融城地下空间开发项目正式开工建设。项目由位于金茂西侧 Z2-1 绿地下 7248 平方米的地下建筑、地面绿化景观以及与周边地标性建筑相连的 5 条地下通道共同组成。项目占地面积 1.35 万平方米，地面绿化景观面积 1.23 万平方米，地下建筑为 2 层，主要为人行集散中心与少量辅助性商业设施。该项目计划于 2015 年年初竣工。

6

SUPPORTING ENVIRONMENT

配套环境

FREE WI-FI SERVICE ARRIVES IN THE CORE AREA OF LUJIAZUI FINANCIAL CITY
陆家嘴金融城中心区实现"CMCC-LJZ"等免费 WIFI 全覆盖
LUJIAUZI TALENT APARTMENTS OPENS
陆家嘴金融城人才公寓启用
LED SCREEN FEATURING FINANCIAL MARKET NEWS INSTALLED
金融行情"登陆"陆家嘴人行天桥
"LUJIAZUI" MAGAZINE LAUNCHED IN LUJIAZUI FINANCIAL CITY
《陆家嘴》杂志创刊仪式在陆家嘴金融城举行
SHUTTLE BUS AND NEW BUS ROUTES LAUNCHED
陆家嘴金融城 2 路、3 路和人才公寓专线 3 条短驳巴士开通
ENGLISH WEBSITE OF LUJIAZUI FINANCIAL DISTRICT LAUNCHED
陆家嘴金融城英文网站开通
MOBILE CATERING CARS COMPLETED
陆家嘴金融城完善白领便捷式餐饮点
......

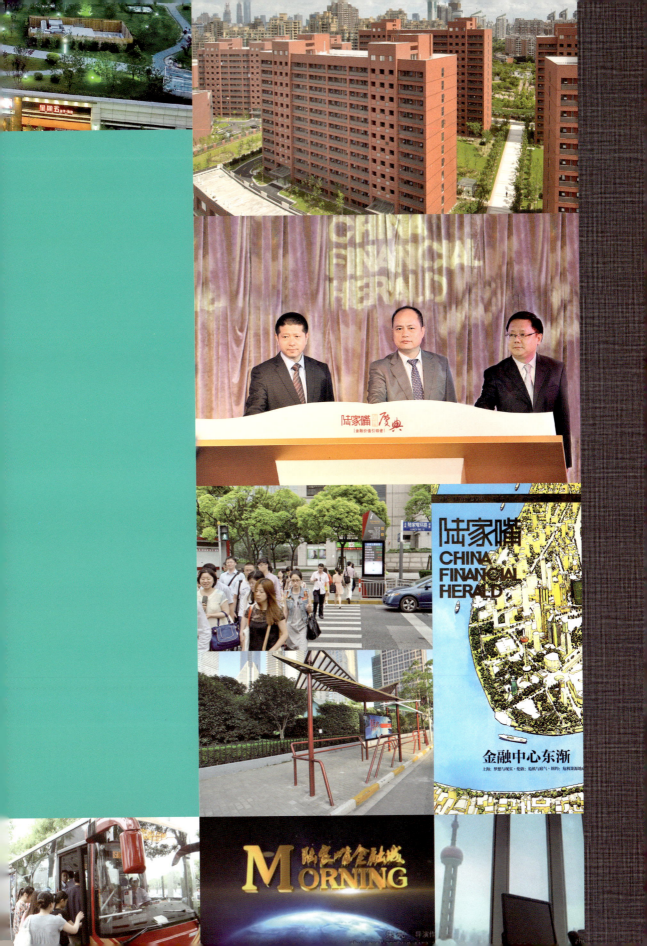

2013

LUJIAZUI FINANCIAL &
TRADE ZONE YEARBOOK
2013陆家嘴金融城年鉴
Abridged Version | 中英对照简缩版

配套环境
SUPPORTING ENVIRONMENT

NO.6

2012-2-2

FREE WI-FI SERVICE ARRIVES IN THE CORE AREA OF LUJIAZUI FINANCIAL CITY

▶ February 2 – Free Wi-Fi coverage was activated in Lujiazui, covering 30 major commercial buildings, the South Riverside recreational areas and other public places. Mobile terminals will allow the public to enjoy high-speed internet connections in Lujiazui.

陆家嘴金融城中心区实现 "CMCC-LJZ" 等免费 WIFI 全覆盖

2月2日，南滨江地区等公共休闲场所、小陆家嘴区域内近 30 栋主要商务楼宇已实现 "CMCC-LJZ" 等免费 Wi-Fi 全覆盖，市民可通过便携终端实现高速网络公共信息化服务。

1
Provided by ORUN
供图 /ORUN

2 3
Photographer / Yao Jianliang
摄影 / 姚建良

LUJIAUZI TALENT APARTMENTS OPENS

▶ March 15 – The Lujiazui Talent Apartments officially opened. It contains 2386 units, of which 1764 are open for occupation. Working professionals who rent apartments there are eligible for the "631" rent subsidy policy provided by the Lujiazui Finance and Trade Zone Management Committee and the rent can be also be covered by their housing allowances. There is shuttle bus service between the apartment complex and Lujiazui Financial City. As of the end of 2012, 1694 apartment units had been rented, accounting for 71% of the total rentals among similar residences in Shanghai. Additionally, the Lujiazui Talent Apartments won the Most Popular Housing Award prize at the municipal competition "My Favorite Affordable Housing Design." This victory proves the success of the "tailor-made" apartment model that allows tenants to customize units to their liking.

陆家嘴金融城人才公寓启用

3月15日，陆家嘴金融城人才公寓正式开业运营。该项目共有单身公寓、大户型公寓共2386套，全年已分批推出1764套。租赁公寓的金融白领可享受陆家嘴金融贸易区管委会提供的"631"租金梯度补贴政策，并可支取公积金支付房租，人才公寓至金融城还开通了往返短驳巴士，为人才提供实实在在的优惠政策和便利的生活配套。截至年底，公寓已完成出租1694套，整体出租率达71%。这一租赁势头堪列本市人才公寓项目的首位；同时，人才公寓还在"我最喜欢的保障房设计评选"（市级评选）中荣获最受欢迎房型奖。这些都充分证明，"度身定制、拎包入住"的创新公寓模式已得到人才和市场的肯定。

中小板综　5971.78　-2.14%　-130.81　2013-10-25　15:00:34　法兰克福
沪铜　　　51150.00　-1.03%　　　　-530　2013-10-25　15:16:32　FRANKFURT

2013

LUJIAZUI FINANCIAL &
TRADE ZONE YEARBOOK
2013陆家嘴金融城年鉴
Abridged Version | 中英对照简缩版

配套环境
SUPPORTING ENVIRONMENT

NO.6

1
Photographer / Gao Jie
摄影 / 高洁

2
Photographer / Wei Shile
摄影 / 魏诗乐

2012-5-22

LED SCREEN FEATURING FINANCIAL MARKET NEWS INSTALLED

▶ May 22, A large LED screen on the pedestrian overpass at Lujiazui began scrolling the latest financial news from the world's major financial markets. The addition of the LED screen will help Lujiazui boost its brand brand image, facilitate the construction of an international financial center in Sanghai and help the area's working professionals stay abreast of the latest happenings in global financial markets.

金融行情"登陆"陆家嘴人行天桥

5 月 22 日，在陆家嘴人行天桥的 LED 屏上，开始滚动播放全球主要金融市场的最新财经资讯。据悉，这是陆家嘴打造金融城品牌，推进国际金融中心软环境建设的一个新尝试，希望借此进一步营造金融城的金融文化氛围，也方便了在附近工作的白领们及时了解世界财经动态。

2013

LUJIAZUI FINANCIAL &
TRADE ZONE YEARBOOK
2013陆家嘴金融城年鉴
Abridged Version | 中英对照简缩版

配套环境
SUPPORTING ENVIRONMENT

NO.6

1 2
Provided by ORUN
供图 /ORUN

2012-6-27

"LUJIAZUI" MAGAZINE LAUNCHED IN LUJIAZUI FINANCIAL CITY

▶ June 27 – The "Lujiazui" Magazine was launched in the Lujiazui Financial City. Co-published by CBN and the Lujiazui Finance and Trade Zone Management Committee, the magazine will help boost the "Lujiazui" brand. It is aimed at a readership of high net-worth individuals and financial institutions. Vice Chairman of the Shanghai Political Consultative Committee and Pudong New District Governor Jiang Liang, Pudong New District Standing Committee Member and Vice Mayor Yan Xu and Pudong New District Committee Member and Publicity Minister Deng Jie attended the opening ceremony. Overall, more than 200 people from the financial sector also attended the event.

《陆家嘴》杂志创刊仪式在陆家嘴金融城举行

6月27日，《陆家嘴》杂志创刊仪式在陆家嘴金融城举行。《陆家嘴》杂志是第一财经与陆家嘴金融贸易区管理委员会共同出品，将有助于金融城品牌建设。《陆家嘴》杂志主要面向金融机构和高净值资产人士，致力于报道具有行业旗帜意义的金融机构、金融家以及重要事件。上海市政协副主席、区长姜樑，浦东新区区委常委、副区长严旭，浦东新区区委常委、宣传部长邓捷等出席，200多名金融界人士参加活动。

Provided by IC Press
供图 /IC Press

2
Photographer / Wei Shile
摄影 / 魏诗乐

LUJIAZUI FINANCIAL &
TRADE ZONE YEARBOOK
2013陆家嘴金融城年鉴
Abridged Version | 中英对照简缩版

配套环境
SUPPORTING ENVIRONMENT

NO.6

2012-6-28

SHUTTLE BUS AND NEW BUS ROUTES LAUNCHED

▶ June 28 - Lujiazui Financial City bus routes 2 and 3 and a shuttle bus that travels between the Lujiazui Talent Apartments were launched. The city buses and shuttle buses provide transportation coverage for the entire Lujiazui area.

陆家嘴金融城 2 路、3 路和人才公寓专线 3 条短驳巴士开通

6 月 28 日，陆家嘴金融城 2 路、3 路和人才公寓专线 3 条短驳巴士开通。至此，陆家嘴金融城公交短驳巴士实现了金融贸易核心区交通枢纽至重要楼宇的全覆盖。

2013

LUJIAZUI FINANCIAL &
TRADE ZONE YEARBOOK
2013陆家嘴金融城年鉴
Abridged Version | 中英对照简缩版

配套环境
SUPPORTING ENVIRONMENT

NO.6

1 2
Provided by ORUN
供图 /ORUN

2012-8

ENGLISH WEBSITE OF LUJIAZUI FINANCIAL DISTRICT LAUNCHED

▶ The English website of the Lujiazui Financial District was launched. The site aims to inform investors, both domestic and foreign, about the benefits of investing in Lujiazui, attract more investment from the world's top companies and strengthen the Lujiazui brand. In 2012, China Daily regularly updated the Luijiazui English website and made changes to142,000 words and the site received 210,000 visits. Additionally, articles from the website were re-published a number of times by foreign media in the United Kingdom, the United States, Singapore and other countries, helping more people overseas become familiar with Lujiazui. This has important implications for the development of an international financial center in Shanghai.

陆家嘴金融城英文网站开通

陆家嘴金融城英文网站是一个主要面向投资者和海内外关心陆家嘴金融城建设与发展人士的网站。目的是推动陆家嘴金融城国际品牌建设，吸引更多优质企业入驻。根据不完全统计，截至年底，陆家嘴金融城英文网站更新字数 14.2 万字，网站累计访问量约 21 万人次。网站部分文章被英国、美国、新加坡等境外媒体多次转载，受到海内外人士青睐，对上海国际金融中心建设具有重要意义。

2012-8-16

SUNSHINE READING ROOMS ESTABLISHED

▶ August 16 - Pudong Library set up the "Sunshine Reading Room" in the lobbies of the "Lujiazui Jiangong Building, Times Financial Center, World Plaza and CIMIC Tower, respectively. Each "Sunshine Reading Room" has 500-1000 books for working professionals to read free of charge.

浦东图书馆在陆家嘴建工大厦、时代金融中心、世界广场、斯米克大厦底楼大厅首设"阳光阅读吧"

8月16日，浦东图书馆在陆家嘴建工大厦、时代金融中心、世界广场、斯米克大厦底楼大厅首设"阳光阅读吧"，每个"阅读吧"都配置了500册至1000册图书，供白领免费借阅。

2013

LUJIAZUI FINANCIAL &
TRADE ZONE YEARBOOK
2013陆家嘴金融城年鉴
Abridged Version | 中英对照简缩版

配套环境
SUPPORTING ENVIRONMENT

NO.6

1
Photographer / Wei Shile
摄影 / 魏诗乐

2 3
Photographer / ORUN
摄影 /ORUN

2012-8

SOUTH RIVERSIDE BAR STREET PROJECT COMPLETED

▶ In late August, the South Riverside Bar Street project was completed. The project is part of a large riverside revival plan spanning 4,360 square meters that also includes the renovation of Fucheng Road Leisure Street and the addition of new retail shops. Additional comprehensive renovation will occur south of West Lujiazui Road, east of Riverside Avenue and west of Fucheng Road. There, a construction project comprising 14,600 square meters, including a dedicated commercial area of 1,650 square meters will be built. Furthermore, the Fucheng Road Leisure Street project, spanning a total area of 1,087 square meters, will be located on the south side of Shibu Road and north of Huayuanshiqiao Road and will include casual dining, bars and teahouses. Lastly, the commercial facility project located north of Tomson Riviera, east of the Lujiazui Ring Road and west of Fucheng Road, will span a total of 1623 square meters and showcase European-style architecture.

南滨江酒吧休闲街项目完成

8月底，南滨江酒吧休闲街项目完成。项目由南滨江三角地综合改造工程、富城路休闲街和商业配套设施建设等3个项目所组成，全部建成后将新增商业配套面积约4360平方米。综合改造工程位于陆家嘴西路南侧，滨江大道东侧，富城路西侧，由园林绿化、地下停车库、人行天桥、公交车站和配套商业5部分组成，总建筑面积14600平方米，其中配套商业面积为1650平方米。富城路休闲街项目位于富城路西侧，南至拾步街，北至花园石桥路，建设2幢单层临街商业配套用房，总建筑面积1087平方米，将以酒吧、茶吧等休闲餐饮类设施为主。商业配套设施项目，北侧紧临汤臣一品，东至陆家嘴环路，西至富城路，总建筑面积约1623平方米，为一幢独立的欧式风格建筑，将被打造成与周边环境相配套的中高档休闲餐饮场所。

2013

LUJIAZUI FINANCIAL &
TRADE ZONE YEARBOOK
2013陆家嘴金融城年鉴
Abridged Version | 中英对照简缩版

配套环境
SUPPORTING ENVIRONMENT

NO.6

1
Photographer / Wei Shile
摄影 / 魏诗乐

1

2012-9

MOBILE CATERING CARS COMPLETED

In September, the Lujiazui Finance and Trade Zone Commission optimized the cars for maximum efficiency, adjusting their routes to coincide with those taken by the Lujiazui Financial City shuttle bus lines. There will be 3 more catering venues added in the future.

陆家嘴金融城完善白领便捷式餐饮点

9月，陆家嘴金融贸易区管理委员会完成了对便捷式餐饮点项目的完善调整。主要包括：移动式餐饮车点位结合陆家嘴金融城短驳巴士线路进行布点。原有的9个点位根据经营情况调整布点位置，并增设3个点位，共计12个移动式餐饮点15辆餐饮车。

2

3

2 **3** **4**
Provided by ORUN
供图 / ORUN

SHORT FILM "MORNING LUJIAZUI" COMPLETED

▶ December 6 – The short film "Morning Lujiazui" was completed and began broadcasting online. The film highlights Lujiazui's many virtues, including its soaring skyscrapers, world-class financial institutions, sweeping rIver views and lush greenbelt as well as explains its recent achievements and future prospects. The film aims to attract greater attention for Lujiazui from the international community.

陆家嘴金融城形象宣传片微电影《Morning 陆家嘴》摄制完成

　　12 月 6 日创作完成微电影《Morning 陆家嘴》，通过网络广泛推广，让公众感受金融城摩天大厦、金融机构集聚、无敌江景、惬意漫步绿地，了解陆家嘴金融城近年来的发展与成就，吸引世界目光聚焦陆家嘴、投身陆家嘴、建设陆家嘴。

7

CULTURE
文化

2012 LUJIAZUI FINANCIAL CITY ARCHERY WORLD CUP
2012 "陆家嘴金融城杯" 射箭世界杯（上海站）落幕
FOURTH TRILATERAL MEETING OF CULTURE MINISTERS
第四次中日韩文化部长会议在上海国际会议中心举行
LUJIAZUI CULTURE AND ART FESTIVAL
陆家嘴金融城开展 "上海一圈" 青年文化活动
"SHANGHAI SUMMER CHARM" CONCERT
"上海·夏之魅" 城市景观交响音乐会
THE 3rd SHANGHAI SUMMER MUSIC FESTIVAL
第三届上海夏季音乐节在陆家嘴中心绿地举行
SIXTH LUJIAZUI FINANCE CULTURE FESTIVAL
第六届陆家嘴金融文化节开幕
2012 SHANGHAI MIDI ELECTRONIC MUSIC FESTIVAL
2012 上海迷笛电子音乐节开幕
THE 2nd PUDONG CULTURE AND ART FESTIVAL CONCLUDES
第二届浦东文化艺术节在东方艺术中心闭幕
SHANGHAI DESIGN WEEK KICKS OFF
2012 上海设计之都活动周开幕
……

2013

LUJIAZUI FINANCIAL &
TRADE ZONE YEARBOOK
2013陆家嘴金融城年鉴
Abridged Version | 中英对照简缩版

文化
CULTURE

NO.7

2012-1-1

2012 NEW YEAR'S DAY CLIMB

▶ A climbing event to mark the start of 2012 was held at the Oriental Pearl Tower. Climbers included more than 1,200 people from all walks of life who were divided up into four groups that marched to the top of the tower.

2012 元旦登高迎新年活动

　　1月1日，"新起点，新年步步高"2012元旦登高迎新年活动在年东方明珠举行。来自社会各界的1200多名选手分成4个组分别在东方明珠塔下向塔顶进发。

1

Provided by Shanghai Oriental Pearl TV Tower
供图 / 上海东方明珠广播电视塔

2012-1-15—3-10

2012 PLUM EXHIBITION HELD AT CENTURY PARK

▶ Jan. 15 to March 10 - Century Park hosted the "2012 Plum Exhibition." The exhibition area totaled 200,000 square meters, with the main scenic area measuring 50,000 square meters. More than 100 species of plums trees and 10,000 overall trees were displayed as well more than 500 potted bonsai trees. Nearly 134,000 visitors attended the exhibition.

2012 年梅花蜡梅展在世纪公园举办

　　1 月 15 日—3 月 10 日，世纪公园举办了"2012 年梅花蜡梅展"展出区域面积达 20 万平方米，主景区近 5 万平方米，共有梅花蜡梅古树 100 余株、地栽梅花蜡梅近 10000 株、梅花和蜡梅树桩盆景 500 余盆。共接待游客近 13.4 万人次。

1
Provided by Century Park
供图 / 世纪公园

2
Photographer / Li Yonggang
摄影 / 李永刚

2013

LUJIAZUI FINANCIAL &
TRADE ZONE YEARBOOK
2013 陆家嘴金融城年鉴
Abridged Version | 中英对照简缩版

文化
CULTURE

NO.7

2012-2-16

LARGE RETROSPECTIVE FOR 14th FINA WORLD CHAMPIONSHIPS

▶ February 16 - A major retrospective of the 14th FINA World Championships was held on the 4.2 meter City Promenade of the Oriental Pearl Tower. The exhibition included five different parts – "Leading Care," "Inside and Outside the Stadium," "Champion Style," "Unforgettable Moments," "Fun Trivia," and more than 200 pictures from the event taken by Xinhua News Agency photographers on the ground, underwater and aerially as well as a three-dimensional reproduction of the event. The retrospective was presented by the 14th FINA World Championships Organizing Committee and co-organized by the Shanghai Sports Bureau and Xinhua News Agency Shanghai Bureau.

第 14 届国际泳联世界锦标赛大型回顾展

2 月 16 日，以"泳动东方·水的礼赞"为主题的第 14 届国际泳联世界锦标赛大型回顾展在东方明珠塔 4.2 米城市长廊展出。展览包括前言和"领导关怀"、"赛场内外"、"冠军风采"、"精彩瞬间"和"缤纷花絮"等 5 个部分，展示了新华社记者拍摄的 200 多幅赛事图片，图片采用空中、水下、陆地三位一体模式拍摄，立体再现了一届精美绝伦的游泳世锦赛。展览由第 14 届国际泳联世界锦标赛组委会、上海市体育局、新华社上海分社共同主办。

3
Provided by Shanghai Oriental Pearl TV Tower
供图 / 上海东方明珠广播电视塔

4
Provided by IC Press
供图 /IC Press

2013

LUJIAZUI FINANCIAL &
TRADE ZONE YEARBOOK
2013陆家嘴金融城年鉴
Abridged Version | 中英对照简缩版

文化
CULTURE

NO.7

2012-4-14—4-15

2012 LUJIAZUI FINANCIAL CITY ARCHERY WORLD CUP

▶ April 14 to 15, 2012 – The Lujiazui Financial City Archery World Cup tournament concluded on Riverside Avenue. 51 countries and regions and 370 players and coaches participated in the tournament. The preliminary and elimination rounds were held from April 10 to 13 at the Yuanshen Sports Center. There were the following types of competition in the tournament: individual men's, individual women's, single-sex groups, mixed groups, individual women's compound bow, single-sex group and mixed group. The Chinese team defeated the U.S. team 143 to 141 to capture the bronze medal.

2012"陆家嘴金融城杯"射箭世界杯（上海站）落幕

4月14日—15日, 2012"陆家嘴金融城杯"射箭世界杯(上海站)的比赛在滨江大道落幕。本次比赛共有51个国家和地区的370名运动员、教练员报名。4月10日—13日的预赛和淘汰赛在浦东源深体育中心进行，决赛在滨江大道进行，共产生反曲弓男女个人、团体、混合团体，复合弓男女个人、团体和混合团体10枚金牌；中国队以143环比141环战胜美国队夺得铜牌。

1 2 3
Photographer / ORUN
摄影 /ORUN

4
Photographer / Xue Chunhui
摄影 / 薛春会

2013

LUJIAZUI FINANCIAL &
TRADE ZONE YEARBOOK
2013陆家嘴金融城年鉴
Abridged Version | 中英对照简缩版

文化
CULTURE

NO.7

2012-5-5

FOURTH TRILATERAL MEETING OF CULTURE MINISTERS

▶ May 5 - The Fourth Trilateral Culture Ministers Meeting was held at the Shanghai International Convention Center. Chinese Minister of Culture Cai Wu, Japanese Minister of Education, Culture, Sports, Science & Technology, Mr Hirofumi Hirano, Korean Culture, Sports and Tourism Minister Cui Guang Zhi attended the event and signed the "China-Japan-Korea Ministerial Conference on Culture - Shanghai Action Plan (2012-2014), marking the beginning of a new era of trilateral cultural exchange and cooperation. The 3 nations agreed to boost cultural exchanges through various governmental and non-governmental channels.

第四次中日韩文化部长会议在上海国际会议中心举行

5月5日，第四次中日韩文化部长会议在上海国际会议中心举行。中国文化部部长蔡武、日本文部科学大臣平野博文、韩国文化体育观光部长官崔光植出席会议。三方共同签署了《中日韩文化部长会议——上海行动计划（2012年至2014年）》。此次会议的举行，标志着中日韩文化交流与合作进入了新阶段。加强文化艺术、文化产业、文化遗产和非物质文化遗产等领域的交流与合作及政府间协商机制，为三国文化部长定期交换意见提供了良好的平台。

1

1
Provided by Shanghai International Convention Center
供图／上海国际会议中心

2013

LUJIAZUI FINANCIAL &
TRADE ZONE YEARBOOK
2013陆家嘴金融城年鉴
Abridged Version | 中英对照简缩版

文化
CULTURE

NO.7

2012-6-15—10-19

LUJIAZUI YOUTH CULTURE FESTIVAL

▶ June 15 to October 19 - Lujiazui held a total of 10 "Shanghai Circle" youth culture activities on the Lujiazui Greenbelt. The activities included "The Thousand Friends Circle," "Creative Charity Circle," "Moonlight Literary Circle," "Fashion Trends Circle" and "Gourmet Circle." The event was sponsored by the Baosteel Group, People's Bank, HSBC, Bank of Communications, Fudan University and other 50 organizations and co-organized by the Lujiazui Finance and Trade Zone Management Committee.

陆家嘴金融城开展"上海一圈"青年文化活动

6月15日—10月19日，陆家嘴金融城共开展 10 期"上海一圈"青年文化活动，活动在陆家嘴中央绿地举行。主题活动划分为"千人交友圈"、"创意公益圈"、"月光文艺圈"、"潮流时尚圈"、"美食文化圈"等 5 个主题区域。集青年交友、娱乐文化、社会公益等功能为一体。活动由宝钢集团、人民银行、汇丰银行、交通银行、复旦大学等 50 家单位发起组织，由陆家嘴金融贸易区管委会协办。

1

Provided by Wang Zhanjiang

供图 / 王战江

2

Provided by IC Press

供图 /IC Press

2013

LUJIAZUI FINANCIAL &
TRADE ZONE YEARBOOK
2013陆家嘴金融城年鉴
Abridged Version | 中英对照简缩版

文化
CULTURE

NO.7

2012-7-21

"SHANGHAI SUMMER CHARM" CONCERT

▶ July 21 – The "Shanghai Summer Charm" urban landscape symphonic concert was held at the Oriental Pearl Tower. The theme of the concert was film music and the Shanghai Philharmonic Orchestra played music from more than 10 classic and foreign films and also conducted film screenings. The symphony was organized by the Shanghai Municipal Culture, Radio Broadcasting, Film and Television Administration and Shanghai Radio and Television Station.

"上海·夏之魅"城市景观交响音乐会

7月21日，"上海·夏之魅"城市景观交响音乐会在东方明珠塔举行。此次交响音乐会以电影音乐为主体，上海爱乐乐团演奏了10余部经典中外电影音乐，还进行了交响乐基础知识普及和经典电影放映。本次交响音乐会由上海市文广局、上海广播电视台主办。

1 2
Photographer / Xue Chunhui
摄影 / 薛春会

3
Provided by Shanghai Oriental Pearl TV Tower
供图 / 上海东方明珠广播电视塔

2013

LUJIAZUI FINANCIAL &
TRADE ZONE YEARBOOK
2013陆家嘴金融城年鉴
Abridged Version | 中英对照简缩版

文化
CULTURE

NO.7

1 Provided by IC Press
供图 /IC Press

2012-7-26—8-12

LARGE PAPER ART EXHIBITION AT IFC

July 26 to August 12- A large paper art exhibition debuted on the first floor of the IFC Mall, featuring three-dimensional renderings of landmarks. All paper works of art on display were done by four internationally-renowned masters: Alexan der Korzer Robinson, Christina Lihan, Jennifer Khoshbin and Sher Christopher.

大型纸艺术展亮相国金中心商场一楼

7月26日—8月12日，大型纸艺术展亮相上海国金中心商场一楼，立体呈现大洋彼岸伦敦的标志性建筑。展出的所有纸艺术作品均出自 4 位国际大师之手，包括 Alexan der Korzer Robinson、Christina Lihan、Jennifer Khoshbin、Sher Christopher。

165

2013

LUJIAZUI FINANCIAL &
TRADE ZONE YEARBOOK
2013陆家嘴金融城年鉴
Abridged Version | 中英对照简缩版

文化
CULTURE

NO.7

2012-7-29—8-12

THE 3rd SHANGHAI SUMMER MUSIC FESTIVAL

▶ July 29 to August 12, 2012 - The Shanghai Summer Music Festival was held on the Lujiazui Greenbelt. There were a total of 35 musical performances. 2 of them were orchestral, while there were 3 symphonies, 4 choir performances and 8 ensemble performances. Additionally, 9 conductors performed, along with 23 dancers. More than 700 artists attended the performance and the festival attracted some 20,000 spectators.

第三届上海夏季音乐节在陆家嘴中心绿地举行

7月29日—8月12日，2012上海夏季音乐节在陆家嘴中心绿地举行。本届夏季音乐节由上海交响乐团与浦东新区人民政府、黄浦区人民政府共同主办。音乐节期间总共35场音乐会中，参演艺术家来自世界各地的2个驻节乐团、3个交响乐团、4个合唱团，8个重奏团，9位中外指挥家以及23位中外独奏、独唱家和舞者等，参演总人数将近700人。音乐节共吸引2万余人次观众参与。

2013

LUJIAZUI FINANCIAL &
TRADE ZONE YEARBOOK
2013陆家嘴金融城年鉴
Abridged Version | 中英对照简缩版

文化
CULTURE

NO.7

2012-9-21

STRENGTHENING PUBLIC SERVICE

▶ September 21 – The China Public Service Awards were held at the Lujiazui Central Green, co-sponsored by the "First Financial Daily," " China Philanthropy Times " and "Jing Bao." 16 projects were awarded and thousands of professionals attended the event.

"让公益更有力量"公益中国 2012 年度评选上海落幕

9月21日，由《第一财经日报》、《公益时报》以及《晶报》等联合发起的"公益中国"2012 年度评选活动颁奖典礼在陆家嘴中心绿地举行，"公益中国"终审评委、16 家入围项目机构与来自上海一圈的上千名白领参加了此次活动。

1 2 3 4
Provided by Wang Zhanjiang
供图 / 王战江

年度评选
Annual Award

第一财经 SMG
公益时报 CHINA PHILANTHROPY TIMES

合作伙伴

上海壹圈

2013

LUJIAZUI FINANCIAL &
TRADE ZONE YEARBOOK
2013陆家嘴金融城年鉴
Abridged Version | 中英对照简缩版

文化
CULTURE

NO.7

2012-9-30—10-6

13th SHANGHAI INTERNATIONAL MUSIC FIREWORKS FESTIVAL

▶ Sept. 30, Oct. 3 , Oct. 6 , - The 13th Shanghai International Music Fireworks Festival was held at Century Park over a three-day period as part of the Shanghai Tourism Festival. Fireworks masters from China, Canada, Poland, France, Italy and Belgium performed at the festival, and finally the Belgium master got the championship. Sponsored by the Yongda vehicles, the festival was attended by nearly 90,000 visitors.

第十三届上海国际音乐烟花节

9 月 30 日、10 月 3 日、10 月 6 日，在世纪公园镜天湖畔，举办为期 3 天的 2012 上海旅游节——永达之夜第十三届上海国际音乐烟花节。由中国、加拿大、波兰、法国、意大利、比利时等 6 个国家的烟花大师同台表演，最终比利时专场夺得冠军。活动迎来了游客近 9 万人次。

1
Photographer / ORUN
摄影 /ORUN

2013

LUJIAZUI FINANCIAL &
TRADE ZONE YEARBOOK
2013陆家嘴金融城年鉴
Abridged Version | 中英对照简缩版

文化
CULTURE

NO.7

1 2 3
Photographer / Liu Bingbiao
摄影 / 刘炳标

4
Photographer / Gu Binhai
摄影 / 顾宾海

2012-10-17—10-21

INTERNATIONAL FOLK DANCE CULTURAL
CULTURE FESTIVAL HELD AT THE ORIENTAL
PEARL TOWER PLAZA

▶ October 17 to 21- With "Oriental Dance" as the theme,
the International Folk Dance and Culture Festival was
launched at the Pearl Oriental Tower Square. Folk dance
teams from the United States, Ireland, Germany as well
as Shanghai, Xinjiang and Yunnan performed vigorously
for the audience. The performances featured distinctive
dances from the respective countries and regions.

国际民间民俗健身舞蹈大会开幕式及展演活动
在东方明珠塔广场举行

　　10月17日—21日，以"世界风情·曼舞东方"
为主题的国际民间民俗健身舞蹈大会开幕式及展演活动
在东方明珠塔广场举行。来自美国、爱尔兰、德国等国
家以及上海、新疆、云南等地的民间民俗舞蹈团队，为
中外观众表演了极具民族特色和民俗风韵的体育舞蹈。

2013

LUJIAZUI FINANCIAL &
TRADE ZONE YEARBOOK
2013陆家嘴金融城年鉴
Abridged Version | 中英对照简缩版

文化
CULTURE

NO.7

2012-10-19

SIXTH LUJIAZUI FINANCE CULTURE FESTIVAL

▶ October 19 - The Sixth Lujiazui Finance Culture Festival was held from October 19 to November 2 at Shuanghui Plaza. More than 15 events were held during the festival period that began with a long-distance run in which 1,000 runners participated. Other highlights included a financial forum, musical performances by the river, a museum with special exhibitions about the finance industry, a golf tournament and special visits by eminent artists. The festival was jointly organized by the Pudong New Disttrict People's Government, the Pudong New Area Financial Services Bureau and the Lujiazui Finance and Trade Zone of Lujiazui Financial City.

第六届陆家嘴金融文化节开幕

10月19日，第六届陆家嘴金融文化节在双辉广场开幕，以环金融城千人长跑活动作为开幕式活动。文化节至11月2日结束，期间举办了各类活动15项，包括2012浦东金融人才论坛、陆家嘴金融城名校直通车、舌尖上的金融城、浪漫滨江音乐秀、金融博物馆开放日、金融精英高尔夫球赛、知名画家进金融城等。活动由由浦东新区人民政府发起，浦东新区金融服务局和陆家嘴金融贸易区管委会联合陆家嘴金融城各界共同举办。

1
Photographer / ORUN
摄影 /ORUN

2
Photographer / Hua Jiashun
摄影 / 华家顺

3 **4** **5** **6**
Provided by Lujiazui Finance&Trade Zone
Adiministration of Shanghai
供图 / 陆管委综合处

2013

LUJIAZUI FINANCIAL &
TRADE ZONE YEARBOOK
2013陆家嘴金融城年鉴
Abridged Version | 中英对照简缩版

文化
CULTURE

NO.7

2012-10-22—10-26

2012 NATIONAL CHINESE PAINTING EXHIBITION

▶ October 22 to 26 – The 2012 National Chinese Painting Exhibition was held at the Shanghai International Convention Center. The event was jointly organized by the Chinese Artists Association and the Pudong New Area Publicity Department (Culture, Radio and Television Bureau). The exhibition comprised more than 3,400 works of art from across China, including calligraphy as well as various paintings: landscape, bird and flower and portraits. Exhibition showcases included 240 selected works and 60 outstanding works.

"翰墨新象" 2012 年全国中国画作品展

10 月 22 日—26 日，由中国美术家协会和浦东新区宣传部（文广局）联合主办的"翰墨新象"2012年全国中国画作品展在上海国际会议中心举办。展览共收到来自全国各地的书画作品 3400 余件，涉及山水、花鸟、人物等创作领域。展览集中展示了评选出的 60 余件优秀作品和 240 余件入选作品。

1 **2**
Provided by Shanghai International Convention Center
供图 / 上海国际会议中心

LUJIAZUI FINANCIAL &
TRADE ZONE YEARBOOK
2013陆家嘴金融城年鉴
Abridged Version | 中英对照简缩版

文化
CULTURE

NO.7

2012 SHANGHAI MIDI ELECTRONIC MUSIC FESTIVAL

▶ October 27 -The 2012 Shanghai Midi Electronic Music Festival, the first outdoor festival of its kind in Shanghai, was held on North Riverside Avenue and featured three open-air stages as well as 28 different Chinese and foreign musical performers. This festival is one of the highlights of the Second Shanghai Pudong Culture & Art Festival.

1 2
Provided by IC Press
供图 /IC Press

2012 上海迷笛电子音乐节开幕

　　10 月 27 日，首届上海户外电子音乐节——2012 上海迷笛电子音乐节在北滨江大道开幕，有 3 个露天舞台以及 28 组中外电子音乐人及组合为电音爱好者们演出。本届音乐节是第二届上海浦东文化艺术节的主要演出项目之一。

2013

LUJIAZUI FINANCIAL &
TRADE ZONE YEARBOOK
2013陆家嘴金融城年鉴
Abridged Version | 中英对照简缩版

文化
CULTURE

NO.7

2012-10-27—10-28

14th CHINA SHANGHAI INTERNA-TIONAL ARTS FESTIVAL HELD

▶ October 27 to 28 - The 14th Shanghai China International Arts Festival "Pudong Yangjing Cup" Yangtze River Delta Area Community Tournament was held in Pudong New District on Yangjing Street. 17 outstanding teams from Zhejing, Jiangsu and Shanghai participated.

第十四届中国上海国际艺术节"浦东洋泾杯"长三角地区社区优秀民乐团队邀请赛举行

10月27日—28日，第十四届中国上海国际艺术节"浦东洋泾杯"长三角地区社区民乐团队邀请赛在浦东新区洋泾街道举行。江浙沪地区的17支优秀团队参赛。

1 Provided by IC Press
供图 /IC Press

2013

LUJIAZUI FINANCIAL &
TRADE ZONE YEARBOOK
2013陆家嘴金融城年鉴
Abridged Version | 中英对照简缩版

文化
CULTURE

NO.7

2012-10-31

THE 2ND PUDONG CULTURE AND ART FESTIVAL CONCLUDES

▶ October 31 - The second session of the Culture and Art Festival in the Pudong Oriental Art Center concluded. The festival lasted for two months. It included the following: more than 2,000 branch teams that created 41 activities, 32 specialty activities, 80 cultural activities and the participation of more than 1.2 million people.

第二届浦东文化艺术节在东方艺术中心闭幕

　　10月31日，第二届浦东文化艺术节在东方艺术中心闭幕。本届艺术节历时2个月，2000多支文化团队打造了41个重点活动项目、32个特色活动项目、80多场基层群众性文化活动，参与市民群众达120余万人次。

1

2

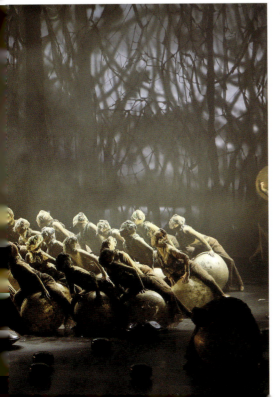

2013

LUJIAZUI FINANCIAL &
TRADE ZONE YEARBOOK
2013陆家嘴金融城年鉴
Abridged Version | 中英对照简缩版

文化
CULTURE

NO.7

2012-11-1

SHANGHAI DESIGN WEEK KICKS OFF

▶ November 1 – The 2012 Shanghai Design Week kicked off at the Shanghai International Convention Center with the theme "Design Illuminating Life." CPPCC Vice Chairman and Revolutionary Committee of the Chinese Kuomintang Vice Chairman Li Wuwei made the keynote speech, touching on themes of "design and urban transformation" and the "Three creates" strategy to accelerate the construction design capital of Shanghai. Shanghai Municipal Committee and Vice Mayor Ai Baojun made the opening speech. 17 Shanghai counties, 89 creative gathering districts and many design companies were present at the event, which attracted 700 people in all.

2012 上海设计之都活动周开幕

　　11 月 1 日，以"设计点亮生活"为主题的 2012 上海设计之都活动周在上海国际会议中心开幕。全国政协副主席、民革中央副主席厉无畏在"设计与城市转型"高峰论坛上作了"以'三创'战略加快推进上海设计之都建设"的主旨演讲。上海市委常委、副市长艾宝俊宣布活动周开幕。上海市 17 个区县、89 个市创意产业集聚区、各类创意设计企业以及历届上海青年高端创意人才约 700 人出席活动。

2013

LUJIAZUI FINANCIAL &
TRADE ZONE YEARBOOK
2013陆家嘴金融贸易区年鉴
Abridged Version | 中英对照简缩版

文化
CULTURE

NO.7

2012-11-2

"AGRICULTURAL BANK OF CHINA NIGHT" SIXTH LUJIAZUI FINANCE YOUTH ARTS CULTURE FESTIVAL

▶ November 2 - The sixth Lujiazui Finance Youth Arts Culture Festival's "ABC Night" was held at the Lujiazui Central Green. Many youths and star actors attended to celebrate the Lujiazui Financial Zone's spirit.

"农行之夜"第六届陆家嘴金融文化节青年文艺汇演举行

11月2日，第六届陆家嘴金融文化节系列活动之——"农行之夜"陆家嘴金融文化节青年文艺汇演在陆家嘴中心绿地举行。来自浦东金融领域的青年和明星演员共同演绎奉献了一台精彩的文艺晚会，展现了陆家嘴金融青年热爱生活和乐观向上的精神风貌。

LUJIAZUI FINANCIAL &
TRADE ZONE YEARBOOK
2013陆家嘴金融城年鉴
Abridged Version | 中英对照简缩版

文化
CULTURE

NO.7

1 2 3
Provided by IC Press
供图 /IC Press

1

2012-11-3

2012 SHANGHAI YOUTH CREA-TIVITY DAY HELD IN CENTURY PARK

▶ November 3 – "Light of Life Design, Creative Change in the Future" Shanghai Youth Creativity Day was held in Century Park as part of Shanghai Design Week for the third consecutive year. The event was co-organized by the Committee of Chinese Communist Youth League, Shanghai Economic Information Committee and, Pudong New District Government.

"设计点亮生活，创意改变未来——2012 上海青年创意日" 活动在世纪公园举行

11 月 3 日，由团市委、市经济信息化委、浦东新区政府共同主办的"设计点亮生活，创意改变未来——2012 上海青年创意日"活动在世纪公园举行，作为 2012 年上海设计之都活动周的重要组成部分，这一活动今年已是连续第三年举办。

2012-11-11

TONY CRAGG SCULPTURE AND PAINTING EXHIBITION

▶ November 11 – The Tony Cragg Sculpture and Painting Exhibition was held at the Shanghai Zenda Himalayas Art Museum. 177 works were displayed, among them 50 sculptures and 127 paintings.

托尼－克拉格雕塑与绘画展在喜玛拉雅美术馆展出

11 月 11 日，托尼－克拉格雕塑与绘画展在上海证大喜玛拉雅美术馆展出。展品包括 50 件雕塑作品和 127 件绘画作品，总计 177 件。

2013

LUJIAZUI FINANCIAL &
TRADE ZONE YEARBOOK
2013 陆家嘴金融城年鉴
Abridged Version | 中英对照简缩版

文化
CULTURE

NO.7

2012-11-18

2012 BWF SUPER SERIES CHINA OPEN ENDS

▶ November 18 – The 2012 BWF Super Series China Open concluded at Yuanshen Stadium. The Chinese team won four championships. There were men's singles finals, women's singles finals and women's doubles. The China Open in 2012 was the 5th tournament held in Yuanshen Stadium. This event has become influential in the world of badminton, according to the first Vice President of the BWF.

2012 年世界羽联超级系列赛中国公开赛落幕

11 月 18 日，2012 年世界羽联超级系列赛中国公开赛在源深体育馆落幕，中国队获 4 项冠军。有男单决赛、女单决赛、女子双打。2012 年是该项国际羽坛顶级赛事落户源深的第 5 年。当大赛落幕，世界羽联第一副主席派山宣布："中国公开赛是 12 站超级系列赛的模版。"中国羽毛球公开赛已成为上海颇有影响的赛事之一。

2 3

Provided by Yuanshen Sports Development Center
供图 / 浦东源深体育发展中心

图书在版编目(CIP)数据

2013陆家嘴金融城年鉴:英文 /《2013陆家嘴金融城年鉴》编委会 编.
—上海:上海三联书店, 2013.11
ISBN 978-7-5426-4404-6

Ⅰ.①2… Ⅱ.①2… Ⅲ.①金融业—浦东新区—2013—年鉴 Ⅳ.①F832.751.3-54

中国版本图书馆CIP数据核字(2013)第239294号

2013陆家嘴金融城年鉴（中英对照简缩版）

主　　编 /《2013陆家嘴金融城年鉴》编委会

责任编辑 / 姚望星
装帧设计 / 史玉新
监　　制 / 李　敏
责任校对 / 张大伟

出版发行 / 上海三联书店
　　　　　（201199）中国上海市都市路4855号2座
　　　　　http://www.sjpc1932.com
　　　　　E-mail:shsanlian @ yahoo.com.cn
设计制作 / 上海傲润平面设计有限公司
印　　刷 / 上海良虹印务有限公司

版　　次 / 2013年12月第1版
印　　次 / 2013年12月第1次印刷
开　　本 / 787×1092　1/16
字　　数 / 30 千字
印　　张 / 12
印　　数 / 1-2000
书　　号 / ISBN 978-7-5426-4404-6/F·657
定　　价 / 150.00元